102 WAYS TO EARN MONEY WRITING 1,500 WORDS OR LESS

I.J. SCHECTER

WRITER'S DIGEST BOOKS

Cincinnati, Ohio
www.writersdigest.com

102 Ways to Earn Money Writing 1,500 Words Or Less. Copyright © 2009 by I.J. Schecter. Manufactured in the United States of America. All rights reserved. No other part of this book may be reproduced in any form or by any electronic or mechanical means including information storage and retrieval systems without permission in writing from the publisher, except by a reviewer, who may quote brief passages in a review. Published by Writer's Digest Books, an imprint of F+W Media, Inc., 4700 East Galbraith Road, Cincinnati, Ohio 45236. (800) 289-0963. First edition.

For more resources for writers, visit www.writersdigest.com/books.

To receive a free weekly e-mail newsletter delivering tips and updates about writing and about Writer's Digest products, register directly at http://newsletters.fwpublications.com.

13 12 5 4 3

Distributed in Canada by Fraser Direct
100 Armstrong Avenue
Georgetown, Ontario, Canada L7G 5S4
Tel: (905) 877-4411

Distributed in the U.K. and Europe by David & Charles
Brunel House, Newton Abbot, Devon, TQ12 4PU, England
Tel: (+44) 1626-323200, Fax: (+44) 1626-323319
E-mail: postmaster@davidandcharles.co.uk

Distributed in Australia by Capricorn Link
P.O. Box 704, Windsor, NSW 2756 Australia
Tel: (02) 4577-3555

Library of Congress Cataloging-in-Publication Data
Schecter, I.J., 1971-
102 ways to make money writing 1,500 words or less / by I.J. Schecter.
p. cm.
ISBN 978-1-58297-795-9 (pbk. : alk. paper)
1. Authorship--Vocation guidance. 2. Authorship--Marketing. I. Title. II. Title: One hundred and two ways to make money writing 1,500 words or less.
PN151.S42 2009
808'.02023--dc22 2009028946

Edited by Melissa Hill
Designed by Terri Woesner
Production coordinated by Mark Griffin

DEDICATION

To my mom and dad, who never once greeted my desire to become a writer with skepticism or alarm. Instead they asked to see my writing, which is the greatest gift a parent can give someone who knows he wants to live in words.

To my sister, for constantly singing my praises to anyone who would listen and acting as my PR manager out of nothing but love and selflessness. She convinced me I was a better writer than I was, which is exactly what I needed to become a better writer.

To my kids, who with one smile supply me the motivation for twenty all-nighters.

To writers everywhere, because:

"If we had to say what writing is we would have to define it essentially as an act of courage." —Cynthia Ozick

"The profession of book-writing makes horse racing seem like a solid, stable business." —John Steinbeck

"It's easy, after all, not to be a writer. Most people aren't writers, and very little harm has come to them." —Julian Barnes

And, as always, to Stephanie. A hundred critics could praise my work and I'd still be nagged by self-doubt; when you praise my work, I feel I can take on the world.

ACKNOWLEDGMENTS

The best part about being asked to write a book about being a writer is getting to talk to so many other writers, established and aspiring, about their thoughts and feelings regarding the writing game.

Yes, I realize there were three "about"s in that last sentence. I believe there were initially four, which tells you why my first thank-you needs to go to the editor of this book, Melissa Hill. Melissa sank her teeth heartily into the manuscript from day one, offering comments like "You aren't saying anything about how to write it or how to sell it." Such comments were unnervingly pertinent when you consider that the book is supposed to be about how to write things and then sell them.

Thanks also to Kelly Nickell, who first came up with the idea for this book and was then generous enough to ask me to write it. I can't think of a greater privilege than being offered the chance to help those trying to make a go of the writing life. I tried to write the book really quickly before Kelly thought of asking someone with better credentials.

Thank you to all of my clients, colleagues, and associates who provided testimonials asserting the value of good writing. Glad you agree.

Finally, my sincere appreciation goes out to the great many writers, in all their wonderful incarnations, who offered comments, anecdotes and insights that helped the book become, I hope, not just a guide but also an affirmation that the freelance life, if approached right, can be a viable one. It was an enormous pleasure to learn the tales of so many freelancers who have taken their shot, stuck with it, and been rewarded. I wish I could have included every single one of their stories.

ABOUT THE AUTHOR

I.J. Schecter is an award-winning writer of fiction, articles, interviews and essays and a highly sought communications consultant serving clients across North America. His recent books include *Slices: Observations from the Wrong Side of the Fairway* and *The Intangibles of Leadership*. I.J. lives in Toronto with his wife Stephanie, his three children, Julian, Oliver and Charlotte, and Oliver's betta fish, Lemon.

TABLE of Contents

INTRODUCTION

For as long as I can remember, I've loved to write. I always kept a pen and pad at my bedside at night. I devoured Archie comics and Danny Dunn books with equal relish. I became incensed with my friends if they didn't faithfully follow the scripts I'd written for the videos we made together. I wrote poems endlessly, thrilled beyond measure to discover that girls could sometimes be moved by my handling of language and tempo. Words were magic, and I longed to know every trick.

Today, I'm lucky enough to call writing my career. Like any successful freelancer, I've been able to reach this point by allowing myself to consider the entire horizon of opportunities available. I've had lots of hits (thank you, *Maxim*!), plenty of misses (come on, *MAD*—my stuff's funny!), and a number of fun surprises (not that I have anything against nudism—I just didn't think I'd ever do a feature on it).

After years of doing this, I still can't predict which queries will make an editor sit up and take notice and which will be discarded faster than you can say, "Good luck placing this elsewhere." But one thing I can say for certain: With professionalism, perseverance, and an open mind, one can make it as a freelance writer.

The purpose of this book is to show you just how broad today's writing landscape is, and thereby help you pursue every possible opportunity in the quest to build your career. At this moment, more prospects exist for freelancers, in more forms, than ever before, and there are a many ways to take advantage of them.

A hundred and two ways, actually. In the following chapters you'll find a great assortment of potential freelance opportunities, along with tips on how to research them and who to contact. Some of these, like magazine features, have no doubt occurred to you; others, like greeting cards, may not. I—or someone I know—have had success with every one of the types of writing discussed in this book. They're real, and they're out there, so don't be afraid to take your shot.

Most important, try to view every opportunity you pursue as part of a long-term, big-picture endeavor. Build relationships. Be willing to market yourself. Stay open to possibilities you may not have thought of before. Act professionally at all times. Freelancing can be challenging, but many people have made it work. You can, too. Good luck!

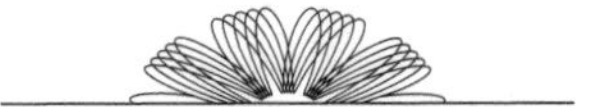

The Top Ten Great Things ABOUT BEING A FREELANCE WRITER

Yvette Adams, internationally successful freelancer

1. The ability to work anywhere. Modern technology means you can be jotting off a story from anywhere with an Internet connection—your mobile phone, an Internet café, or a laptop picking up someone's wireless signal.

2. The chance to meet extraordinary characters. From healers in northern Thailand to a dingo in central Australia that played the piano, I've met some unforgettable people (and other creatures) that have helped make my stories all the richer.

3. The chance to make good of a bad situation. In 1998 I was in Jakarta when President Suharto was overthrown. While I was stuck at the airport for twenty-four hours, I made the most of things by filing a story to my local paper and getting paid for it.

4. The chance to gain access to great events. In 1999 I managed to secure a press pass to cover the Confederations Cup held in Guadalajara, Mexico, a football tournament featuring Brazil, Germany, the United States, and New Zealand. Inside were free food and booze, a welcome sight for a weary backpacker in need of some refreshments! Others (most of them over sixty and male) had waited their entire careers to get into an event like this.

5. The chance to earn cash. At times, freelancing has been my main source of income; at other times it's been supplemental cash for my travels. Either way, it all helps!

6. The chance to travel to new places. In 2001 I pitched a youth travel agency in London telling them that their competitor had a travel agent journeying to different locations and sending back diaries. I scored a free round-the-world trip for a year and a digital camera in exchange for sending back 400 words and four snaps each week.

7. The chance to learn about new places and things. While in Buenos Aires at a bar, I bumped into a woman compiling the Time Out travel guide for Patagonia. One thing led to another and I ended up writing about adventure sports for the publication—not something I can say I knew a lot about before!

8. The chance to see my name in print. Seeing my byline gives me a kick every time.

9. The ability to work from home in my pajamas.

10. The ability to choose my own hours. With two young children, freelancing allows me to choose when and how many hours to work while still being a good mommy.

MAGAZINES

Although I derive a great deal of satisfaction seeing my writing in magazines, it's my wife Stephanie's reaction I always look forward to most. Often after finishing the final draft of an assigned story, I'll hand her the manuscript and ask for comments. I know her feedback will be balanced, because years ago she developed a peerless method for evaluating my work. Passages that work well get a check mark in the margin; those that fall short get a number of comments in red challenging me to do better; those she finds particularly affecting get an "Aww ..."; and those that stand out are denoted by a silhouette of a naked female figure.

No matter how good or bad she thinks the writing is, however, she'll always hand the manuscript back to me with a bit of distaste, and I know why: It looks ugly. All that double-spaced Courier 12-point type, all those double-hyphens for dashes, all those underlines in place of italics—oh, sure, I love it because it's filled with words, but let's face it, aesthetically speaking it's not the Sistine Chapel. "It's good," she'll say, handing it back to me like an unsightly dress I've asked her to try on.

A few months later, when the issue arrives, she'll flip to my article and her eyes will widen. "It's so good," she'll say. "Did you change a lot of it?" Little has been changed, of course—it just looks like a magazine article now.

I share this anecdote to make the point that, yes, there is something impressive about getting your work published in magazines. In the first place, it usually makes for a great tear sheet. In the second place, the pay is, on average, higher than for any other type of noncorporate writing. Finally, it allows you to explore and write about subjects you might never have paid a second thought to before, leading to a continually expanding spectrum of knowledge and expertise you can leverage again and again.

The Landscape

Among the many print markets for freelancers, magazines offer the broadest range of opportunity. There aren't dozens of magazines needing freelance contributors—there are hundreds. Yes, you'll hear people spout doom-and-gloom statistics all the time—the number of magazines that fold every year, the number that can't get enough advertisers, how all of them will eventually be converted to online versions. Ignore the pessimists, okay?

If you need some reassurance, visit your nearest Barnes & Noble and go straight to the magazine section. You won't know where to look first. You've got established big boppers occupying the space they've proudly earned over the course of decades. You've got new titles trying to horn in on that space. And you've got magazines that kind of float beneath the radar, maintaining consistent readership but never threatening to crack the upper levels. Beyond what you see on the local bookstore shelves, you've got everything else: trade journals (bet you didn't know there are half a dozen magazines dedicated just to the stone, quarry, and mining field), regional magazines (there's not only *Alabama Living*, but *Alabama Heritage*, too!), religious publications (more than you'd think—twenty-six pages' worth in the current edition of *Writer's Market*), specialty publications (the *P*s alone yield everything from *Police Times* to *Podiatry Management*), and much, much more, from airline magazines to university publications.

Each magazine has its own requirements, and each magazine editor his own style. But no matter the magazine you're targeting, success comes down to the same set of behaviors: diligent research, precise querying, excellent writing, deadline-hitting, and, not least, being easy to work with. Get enough pitches out there while applying these principles without compromise, and you'll enjoy seeing your byline in magazines for a long time to come.

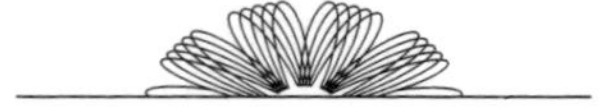

Three Great Magazine Editors ANSWER THREE IMPORTANT QUESTIONS

Q *When querying, what are three common mistakes writers make that lessen their chances for publication?*

Rhonda Bannister, *Queensland Brides*: One: They don't research our title. Two: They send copy for consideration that's obviously written for a newspaper audience. Three: They stalk me with the same style of writing once I have said no because it doesn't suit our parameters.

Jason Sowards, *Golf Illustrated*: One: They have errors and typos in any correspondence with editors. Two: They bombard editors with numerous questions regarding submissions and queries. Three: They submit a query or article that isn't the type we normally publish.

Caroline Connell, *Today's Parent*: One: They deliver a vague topic, not a story idea (e.g., "Why do siblings fight? Talking to parents and experts, I'll explore this subject in 2,000 words ..."). Two: They pitch us on something we did recently (they're not looking at our magazine or Web site). Three: They submit multiple pitches. I've seen several where the writer goofed and forgot to change the magazine's name.

Q *Describe the kind of writer you love to work with. What specific things can a writer do to get on, and stay on, your good side?*

Rhonda Bannister: They turn in excellent, tight copy, nothing sloppy, and do it to the magazine's specifications—not yours. That's what makes you a favorite and why editors will keep coming back to you.

Jason Sowards: We love to work with writers who regularly submit articles that are on time, free of errors, and follow their queries and assignment guidelines. Writers who don't pester the editors with lots of questions or nag about their latest payment will usually stay on our good side.

Caroline Connell: A writer who likes what our publication does, who gets excited about the assigned topic, who delivers on time, and who doesn't assume the editor will take care of the details (e.g., grammar, spelling, factual correctness—you'd be amazed). And, ideally, a writer who appreciates the editor's role, enjoys the dialogue, isn't afraid to express her opinion but wants to deliver what the editor needs.

Q *How do you feel when you receive a bang-on query or a manuscript that nails the assignment?*

Rhonda Bannister: Relieved!

Jason Sowards: When we receive a great query or assignment, it creates an excitement that carries over to all the editors and designers who work on that article. This results in a piece that reaches its full potential and one of which everyone can be proud.

Caroline Connell: Excited! Doesn't happen that often. Makes my proverbial day.

FRONT-OF-BOOK PIECES

Those short bits you see in the first few pages of most magazines are called Front-of-Book (FOB) pieces. Also referred to as quick hits, these brief items serve as warm-ups for the reader, like stepping-stones leading them subtly into the meat of the magazine. Sometimes, quick hits are peppered throughout, like in *Men's Health*. FOB pieces frequently offer the best way for new writers to break into publications because they're low-risk propositions, editorially speaking.

FOB pieces can be as long as a few hundred words or as short as 50. Whatever the length, remember that they represent a proving ground—they're potential springboards toward longer, more prominent stories. In an editor's eyes, someone who can make 150 words sparkle can do the same with 3,000.

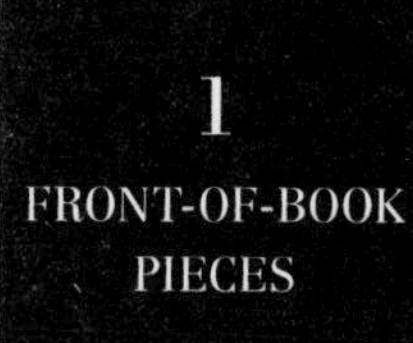

Writing Front-of-Book pieces is a great way for new writers to break into a magazine.

Get This Gig: Front-of-Book Pieces

Where Do I Start?

Get smart on what FOB pieces deliver and the concision with which they do so. For every 250-word FOB item you see, the writer probably amassed enough research for a story ten times that length. I regard FOB stories the way I regard haiku poetry—they may look easy because they're short, but quite the opposite is true. They have structure, rhythm, and energy, and like any longer piece, they give the reader something to think about.

Flip through the past three issues of half a dozen magazines of interest to you and note the kind of things they cover in their FOB pieces. Then start brainstorming.

Who Do I Contact?

If the magazine's listing in *Writer's Market* doesn't indicate which editor to send FOB pieces to, check the masthead and try to obtain contact information for the managing editor or executive editor. Then query away, keeping in mind that a pitch for a short piece ought to be just as good as a pitch for a long one.

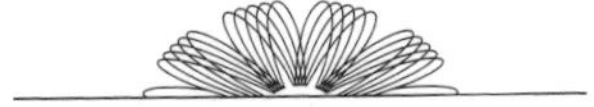

Do You Know Where YOUR STAPLER IS?

Many writers and other artists claim that their extreme lack of organization is simply an occupational hazard. Others practically boast about it, claiming it as a distinct imprint of creativity. Whether or not creative types are naturally disinclined toward orderliness, the sooner you decide to get organized and stay organized, the more successful your practice will become. Why? Two reasons: one physical, the other mental. Physically speaking, when your work environment is organized, you spend more time writing and less time trying to locate the calculator or paper clips or this file or that folder. Simple odds dictate that using your time more productively will lead to more work.

The mental aspect is just as important. We all know how aggravating it is to have to scramble for an important document or try desperately to remember where we put the CD with the backup copy of that contract after the electrical storm has wiped out our operating system with a deadline looming. It stands to reason that the less energy you need to put into nonwriting activities, the more energy you can direct toward your actual work, improving its overall quality and thereby making you a more desirable commodity. Sure, a little anxiety can be healthy for writing, but it should be anxiety born of the drive to produce stellar work, not anxiety based on wondering where the stamps went for the umpteenth time.

Organizing yourself is probably a lot easier than you imagine, and you might even be surprised at how good a little structure makes you feel. Start small: Buy a box of multicolored file folders, some labels, a backup hard drive or memory stick, and several upright magazine files. Label one of the magazine files CONTRACTS, then place in it different file folders labeled with the subject area for a given contract. For me, these folders include, among others, Bridal, Sports & Fitness, Men's, Gardening, and, of course, Writing & Publishing. Label another of the magazine files CURRENT ASSIGNMENTS and a third STORY IDEAS, and populate them as you did the first. Use consistent colors for specific topics—for me, gardening always gets a green file folder whether it's in the STORY IDEAS or the CONTRACTS file. This makes for easy cross-referencing. And that's just a start. Odds are this small bit of organization will spur you to create files for every aspect of your work. "Organization is everything," says freelancer Heather Cook. "From maintaining accurate records for tax purposes to structuring a weekly plan to include marketing and administrative tasks, it allows me to stay focused and efficient—and that makes my overall work better."

ESSAYS

A good number of magazines have a specific page dedicated to essays written by their readers. The most prestigious example of this is the back page of *The New York Times Magazine*, which features a different one-page essay every week by someone you've likely never heard of. Such credits can be great boosts to your portfolio. Years ago I submitted an 800-word piece about watching my son sleep in his crib to *Today's Parent* for its personal essay page. The editors accepted it, and two things happened. First, I became a regular contributor to the magazine. Second, the piece earned some awards, increasing my profile significantly. I've received more comments on that little essay than just about anything else I've ever written.

2
ESSAYS

One of the many examples of essays in magazines is the back page of *The New York Times Magazine*, which features a different one-page essay every Sunday by someone you've probably never heard of.

Get This Gig: Essays

Where Do I Start?

Flip through your favorite magazines to see whether they have something that looks like an essay page. Make your search comprehensive, since essay pages can show up just about anywhere—sometimes on the back page, sometimes near the front, sometimes smack-dab in the middle. Many magazines have the same essay writer all the time; others happily invite submissions. To get this information, check several recent issues of the magazine, inspect its Web site, or review its listing in *Writer's Market*.

Who Do I Contact?

Magazines sometimes have a specific essays editor, which will be noted on the masthead or on the page where the essay appears in the magazine. If you don't see such an editor indicated, send your piece to whatever editor is listed as the contact in *Writer's Market*. If that information isn't available either, but you've seen that the magazine does publish essays, send your manuscript to the managing editor or executive editor.

Writing AGAINST THE GRAIN

Editors are always looking for stories on certain topics—topics referred to as *evergreen*. So you should just find out what those topics are and pitch ideas for them, right?

Not necessarily. One market-cracking technique I've found to be highly useful over the years is writing against the grain. This is different from not writing to trend. Writing to trend means sending pitches about the hot topic of the moment, often an ill-advised practice because the topic is usually gone by the time you get there. Writing against the grain means taking evergreen topics and turning them on their ear. Let me explain.

Being under constant pressure and tight deadlines, editors need evergreen topics because they're safe, reliable, and quick. But these same editors also love having their eyes opened to new possibilities. At one point I became interested in trying to infiltrate the popular golf market, but a slight hurdle was in my way: I'm a terrible golfer. I researched golf magazines wondering what I could add to the abundance of material on lowering handicaps and putting with confidence. Combing through the pages, I was astounded to find that, in all these pages dedicated to what I considered the funniest of sports, virtually no space was allotted to humor. This was all the revelation I needed. My article, "10 Reasons I'll Never Take a Golf Lesson," about why I'm a dreadful golfer and OK with it, was purchased by the now-defunct *Golf Journal* and kick started an ultimately crucial part of my writing career.

The bridal market posed a similar problem. While I'd certainly become familiar with its subject matter during my engagement, all I knew about wedding planning was how stressful it felt. How was I going to break into a market saturated with articles about finding the right dress, writing thank-you cards, and dealing with in-laws? "Write about the groom's perspective," my fiancée advised. "Maybe they'll find it refreshing." She was right. My article, "A Man's Guide to Surviving the Engagement," was purchased by *Brides*, and I became a frequent contributor. Today, when people ask me what kinds of magazines I write for, I still get a kick out of saying, "Oh, you know, golf, fitness, sports ... bridal."

When I decided to target the men's fitness market, I again felt out of my league—I'm the average guy in the gym, inconspicuous on a good day. The magazines in this market were full of behemoths whose pecs, abs, and delts seemed to stand out from the page in high relief. However, few articles spoke to the regular gym goer, the guy who looks more like me than these striated Goliaths. Bucking evergreen topics once again, I wrote an article called "The

Average Guy's Guide to Looking Good at the Gym." *Men's Exercise* bought it. Writing against the grain had worked a third time.

Maybe you're interested in writing for movie magazines. A quick check reveals that they mostly publish reviews of current films, profiles of stars, and all-time-best lists. Step outside the box. What does your experience with movies allow you to write about that hasn't been tapped? Would an article on the different ways people eat popcorn catch an editor's attention? Probably not—the topic is narrow and has only mild entertainment value. On the other hand, a list of the worst male movie hairdos of the past twenty years might be intriguing, since it satisfies a format these magazines are used to but is refreshingly different from the usual lists of best sex scenes or one-liners. Or how about a funny article on why *Top Gun* should be mentioned alongside *Casablanca* among the all-time classics? Or a ranking of the best second bananas ever, like Goose from *Top Gun* and Victor Laszlo from *Casablanca*? That's the other thing about brainstorming against the grain: It's more fun.

 HUMOR

From *Entertainment Weekly* to *Holidays for Couples*, the majority of magazines allot a certain amount of space to articles that are just plain fun. I refer to such pieces as distinct from other articles lighthearted in tone but otherwise information-oriented. A humor piece is identifiable via an easy, one-step test: Its main purpose is to make you laugh (or at least smile). Such pieces are like jugglers; their simple aim is to entertain.

It's important to recognize what's humor and what isn't so you can make it clear to an editor when querying. If you're pitching humor, say so. When I offered "23 Things You Should Never Say on the Golf Course" to *Golf Journal*, I had never actually heard anyone say, "Does anyone know how to get blood off a 9-iron?" so I was making it obvious to them that the strict intention of my piece was to give readers a chuckle. If, on the other hand, you're querying about an educational piece written in a friendly, conversational voice, let the editor know so she's clear about what's being promised.

3 HUMOR	Virtually every magazine has a humor component to it. If it doesn't, maybe you ought to suggest it should.

Get This Gig: Humor

Where Do I Start?

First, read a lot of humorous writing so you understand where the bar is set. Like kids' writing and erotica, funny writing tends to be harder than people assume. Read a few of Dave Barry's columns and, between wiping away tears, study how cleverly Dave takes a universal topic or broadly relevant idea and twists it into his own unique take.

Then, start flipping through magazines. Investigate which have dedicated humor columns. Some are written by the same writer all the time; others use rotating contributors. And don't think that just because a magazine doesn't contain humorous pieces, it isn't open to the suggestion. Sometimes the only reason a magazine doesn't run a humor column is because none of its editors has received the right pitch for one—yet.

Who Do I Contact?

If humor seems to be a staple of the magazine and is given prominent real estate, contact the features editor. Otherwise, try the managing editor or executive editor.

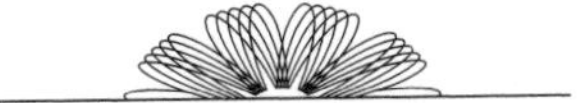

Doing Your HOMEWORK

Every successful freelancer is also a great researcher. Unless you exclusively write first-person essays about your own experiences—which, unless you're Frank McCourt, you probably don't—there's a lot of information you'll need to delve into to properly flesh out the topics you write about. (That's "flesh out," by the way—not "flush out," which is applicable only if you're also trying to get a suspect to come out of hiding.) Editors look for concrete ideas presented from specific angles, not general puffery, and you only get one shot, so you'd better get it right.

Here's the good news: Today, you have no excuse for *not* finding whatever it is you're after. There's a reason this is called the Information Age. If you lived in the Stone Age, imagine saying, "Sorry, I couldn't find any stones." Same applies today. Editors are going to be highly unforgiving toward gaps, ambiguities, or pitches that aren't honed to a fine edge, because anything you need to find is findable.

Here's an example: You have a great story about makeup application techniques that you think would be perfect for the new consumer magazine called *Charm*. (I made that up—don't go looking for it.) Even though *Charm* has a general listing in *Writer's Market*, there's no contact name or number—just the address for their offices and a note saying they rarely accept unsolicited submissions. First off, ignore that. Everybody's looking for good stories all the time. It's just easier for them to include that bit so they don't get inundated with pitches they can't use. But you're convinced that yours is one they *could* use. Well, you don't want to blindly send your pitch into the GAGUS (Great Abyss of Generic Unsolicited Submissions). What's the solution? You need to dig until you have an individual name to send to.

Step one: Make a beeline for the nearest Barnes & Noble and find the current issue of *Charm*. Flip to the masthead, which should list everyone and their dog. Remember there are two mastheads, one for the publishing side of things (this will include people like Vice President of Golfing Three Times per Week) and one for the production side, including editors. That's whom you want to zero in on. You're likely to find a whole gaggle of different editors: executive editor, managing editor, one or more senior editors, features editor, assistant editors and editorial assistants (no, no one knows the difference), and, of course, the grand poo-bah, the editor-in-chief. While the same title can mean different things at different magazines, your best bet is usually to pitch the executive editor or managing editor, who tend to be connected to everyone else in the department.

If that person's contact information isn't listed, there are at least two ways to find it. One way is to call the magazine's offices (the number should be listed at the bottom of the masthead; if not, look it up online or call information) and, when the receptionist answers, pretend you've been given an erroneous e-mail address. For instance: "Oh, hi there. I was just attempting to send Jane Smith at *Charm* an e-mail, but for some reason it's bouncing back. Is her address not jsmith@charm.com?" Usually you'll be dealing with a receptionist who, let's face it, isn't overly focused on security or company policy, so she won't think twice about giving you the information you're after.

Of course, this involves some guesswork. As I said, usually the receptionist will barely hear the e-mail address you've come up with before giving you the right one, but if your guess is too wacky, that same receptionist might turn quickly into the gatekeeper she was hired to be.

There's one double check you can do. If the magazine is owned by a parent company (and nowadays most of them are), check out two or three of the other magazines they publish and see whether the mastheads of any of those magazines list e-mail addresses. The general form (say, firstinitiallastname@publishinggiant.com) is probably the same, or at least similar, at the one you're targeting.

Then, pitch away. Jane Smith doesn't have to know how you got her address—though it's a good bet she'll be impressed that you did. If none of the above works, you can always call the magazine directly, ask for Editorial, and whoever answers, give him the straight-up truth: You have an idea you'd like to pitch and was wondering if he could provide a name and e-mail address for the editor who handles the type of article you're pitching. Sometimes he'll divulge, sometimes he won't. But it's always worth a try.

SERVICE PIECES

Humor pieces are at one end of the spectrum. On the opposite end are service pieces, the term used for articles whose chief purpose is to provide information or to educate readers about a particular subject. For a parenting magazine, a service piece might be about the safest new strollers on the market. For a golf magazine, it might be one covering the top pitching wedges for the upcoming season.

A number of magazines these days are largely service-oriented because that's the most reliable way to draw advertisers, and, consequently, advertising revenue, the primary source of funding for most magazines. Service pieces can involve just about any topic as long as it's current, relevant to the magazine's readership, and accurate. When pitching a service piece, give the editor a reason why you're qualified to write it. Do you work in a store that sells a range of baby equipment, making you a confirmed stroller expert? Are you the manager of a golf course pro shop, giving you exposure to all the different brands of new clubs that come in? Great—let her know!

Service pieces aim to inform readers about a certain topic. Nearly all magazines have a strong need for service pieces because it helps them draw advertisers.

Get This Gig: Service Pieces

Where Do I Start?

Nothing drives an editor batty like receiving a query on a topic that (a) the magazine has just run recently, or (b) doesn't fit with the magazine in the first place. In other words, do your homework; don't guess. Get your hands on a few issues of the magazine you want to query so you can get a feel for the type of service articles they like to run, the kind of format they favor, and the amount of slant or opinion they seem to allow. Then get to work crafting some first-class pitches.

Who Do I Contact?

There's no such thing as a service piece editor, so check first to see if the topic you're writing about belongs to a specific section of the magazine for which there's a dedicated editor. If not, query or submit to the managing editor, executive editor, or deputy editor.

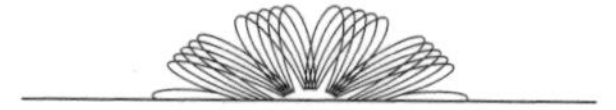

Err on the Side **OF FORMALITY**

With the majority of dialogue between writers and editors now conducted by e-mail, there exists a premature temptation in writers to make editors casual pen pals. Try to feel out the dynamic your editor initiates before writing long e-mails about your mother-in-law's meddling or your guilt over last week's Big Mac indulgence. Let the editor set the tone—jocular or businesslike, expansive or brief—and do your best to match it. Force yourself to consider the timing, content, and tone of any bit of correspondence, which will hopefully lead to a long-standing, mutually beneficial relationship. The relationship may evolve into a more personal one over time, but let it grow naturally rather than trying to force it. During my career, I've become close friends with several editors—our e-mails are typically full of jokes and personal stories. Other editors I've known for years but I still maintain a strict business relationship with them, my queries as straightforward and to the point as they ever were. The relationships you form with editors aren't that different from the relationships you form in every other area of life. The ones you're meant to become friends with, you'll become friends with.

FICTION

Countless writers have started their careers publishing stories in magazines and eventually gone on to greater heights. Magazine fiction continues to be a fertile pasture for tales of every stripe, with an extremely broad spectrum ranging from small-circulation magazines to more familiar newsstand monthlies.

5 FICTION	In the biannual focus groups it conducts with random subscribers, *Esquire* finds its readers tend to single out fiction as one of the top things they look for in the magazine.

Get This Gig: Fiction

Where Do I Start?

Exploring story markets tends to be one of the more fun exercises for writers, and also one of the most daunting simply because there are so many to choose from. If your story falls into a traditional genre, go to the category index in *Novel & Short Story Writer's Market* and look under that genre name for a list of magazines, then check each publication's individual listing to see if your story fits its guidelines. If your story doesn't fall into one of the genre categories, check under Mainstream or Literary in the category index. If you're not sure what category describes your story, go through all the listings and mark the ones—there are many—that simply say they're seeking quality fiction. Like I said, this can be fun, but a little intimidating, too. If you find yourself overwhelmed, take a break and come back to it later.

Who Do I Contact?

In almost every case, magazine listings will include the person to contact for submissions. The smaller the magazine, the more likely that the main contact will be the editor; the larger the magazine, the more likely that the main contact will be the managing editor, executive editor, fiction editor, senior editor, associate editor, literary editor, or editorial assistant. Never attempt to leapfrog the food chain unless someone on the editorial team has specifically requested your submission.

INTERVIEWS/PROFILES

Interviews and profiles are awarded prized space in a number of magazines—think *Vanity Fair's* back page or *Playboy's* main feature. (No, not that main feature—the other one.) Often these pieces are assigned to in-house writers—the bigger the publication, the more probable this is—but there are plenty of magazines that welcome interview or profile pitches from freelancers.

There's no magic formula for accumulating interview credits. You need to learn how to get one crucial thing: access to the interviewee. Sometimes you can obtain it through a single phone call; other times, you need to jump through several hoops to finally get to the person you're after. Naturally, this is most often a function of your subject's level of renown. If you want to profile a restaurateur in your hometown for a local magazine, getting access probably won't prove troublesome, as long as you aren't out to drag him over the coals. If you're trying to land an interview with Brad Pitt, on the other hand, it's going to be more difficult. Remember, though, that difficult doesn't mean impossible. It's *always* worth trying.

The key to building your interview portfolio is gaining access to subjects.

Get This Gig: Interviews/Profiles

Where Do I Start?

Go to the nearest bookstore, take half a dozen magazines off the shelf, and read the interviews or profiles they contain. Don't choose half a dozen of the same type of magazine. Choose magazines of different reaches, with different audiences. Note the structural similarities and differences among the pieces you read. Do the introductions tend to follow a similar pattern and style? Is the writing in some of them more serious and literate and in others more edgy and controversial? Are physical descriptions of the subject always given? In each piece, what theme or angle is the writer using to frame the piece?

Once you've got a feel for the rhythm and structure of interview/profile pieces, think about people you'd like to write about, and why. Editors want stories about those making news. Go get them.

Who Do I Contact?

Before pitching any editors, make contact with your interview subject. Sometimes this will prove harder than you think, sometimes surprisingly easy. Predicting a subject's willingness and accessibility is enormously difficult; it has little to do with your credentials and more to do with the disposition of the person you're trying to interview.

Be specific when you make contact. E-mailing Halle Berry's manager saying "I'd like to interview Halle about anything interesting that's going on with her at the moment" is not going to win you access. But "I'd like to interview Halle for *Ebony* magazine about her journey to stardom, her favorite roles, and her views on the status of black actresses in Hollywood today" stands a better chance.

Once you have access confirmed, craft your pitch. Be clear that your subject has agreed to the interview and indicate how swiftly you can deliver the finished piece.

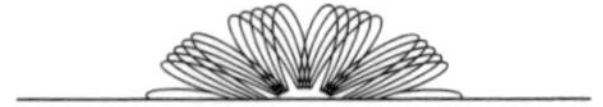

The Publisher of a Cool Guitar Magazine GIVES HIS TOP EIGHT SUBMISSION TIPS

Jason Verlinde, publisher, ***The Fretboard Journal***

1. **My biggest pet peeve is getting a pitch from someone who clearly hasn't read the magazine.** We publish a niche magazine for guitar collectors and enthusiasts, with no instruction. Yet we still get pitches on instruction all the time.

2. **About 30 percent of our content comes from folks who have probably never been published before.** As a new writer, focus on what you know better than anyone else and pitch accordingly.

3. **Please don't call us out the blue.** Send the editor an e-mail and we'll eventually get to it and tell you what we think.

4. **Don't e-mail us a pitch with a bunch of attached clips; we probably won't read more than the first graf or two of the first one.** Instead, send a few links to your favorite examples of your work on the Web, and take the time to write an intelligent introduction and explanation of why you should be writing what you're proposing.

5. **Mentioning an article or two we've actually run is an instant icebreaker.** Saying you "love the magazine and would be a good fit" sounds like you've never read our title and are just looking for work. We already have writers in our stable who are dying for more work. You need to stand out and tell us why you matter.

6. **Meet deadlines, be prompt, and don't make excuses for tardiness.**

7. **Pitch a story you can write right now.** Your first pitch shouldn't be to interview a rock star you don't have any contact with.

8. **Our magazine is photo-heavy, so take the time to think about the finished product and how your piece would be designed.** Will you submit photos? Are you married to a professional photographer? Do you have access to the subjects we could photograph with our staffers? Make things easy on us. If your article has no conceivable visuals, we can't run it.

LISTS

Editors are partial to lists because they're straightforward, tidy, and easy for readers to digest. From *Cosmopolitan* to *Shutterbug*, most magazine covers will probably include at least one headline announcing "Ten Tips for a Mind-Blowing Orgasm," "The Five Best New Digital Cameras," or the like.

When pitching a list article, be clear that it *is* a list. Editors accept pitches based not just on the originality and relevance of the idea but also on its intended structure and format. When they say yes, they're usually already thinking about how your story is going to fit within the overall editorial mosaic of a given issue months down the road. One or two list pieces usually serve as accents to the dish, but rarely are they the entrée, so make sure an editor knows what part of the meal you're offering.

Also, don't think list pieces warrant less-polished queries just because they seem simpler in nature. Lists are critical keystones for all editors, so pitch them just as professionally as you would any other story. Nor should you see them as dull or lackluster. Think of them instead as solid foundations from which lots of creative possibilities can emerge.

When you're querying about a list piece, indicate its format clearly so the editor can visualize where it might fit into the mix.

Get This Gig: Lists

Where Do I Start?

List pieces can take a variety of forms—humorous, informative, scholarly, controversial—so browse many different magazines and read all the different lists you come across. There will be plenty. Then start to think about what kind of list you could put together that the magazine, and its readers, would find relevant and entertaining.

Who Do I Contact?

Aim for one of the editors on the masthead. It's even okay to send your query to an assistant editor. If she likes your idea and brings it to a senior editor, and he likes it, too, she looks like someone who can spot talent, and you've just made *two* important friends.

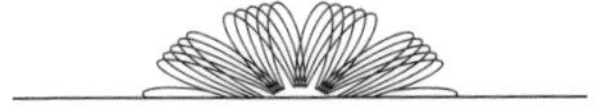

A Word About **ASSISTANT EDITORS**

They aren't going to be assistant editors forever. They're going to be editors, executive editors, managing editors, and editors-in-chief. So treat them with as much courtesy and professionalism as you would anyone higher up the food chain.

QUIZZES

While not quite the staple lists are, quizzes find their way into magazine pages on a regular basis. Editors love them because they're entertaining, informative, and engaging. Readers love them for the same reasons. Quizzes are also somewhat simpler in execution than other types of stories because, though they do require good research and a logical flow, they're straightforward in structure. Finally, they're a great way for you to demonstrate a variety of different skills to an editor. Submitting one great quiz can show that you're organized, thorough, know how much to leave in and how much to leave out, and can inform and entertain at the same time.

Quizzes offer a great way for readers to actively engage with the magazine. Try to make your quiz easy enough for readers to feel they're well informed but challenging enough for them to feel they've learned a thing or two.

Get This Gig: Quizzes

Where Do I Start?

Before pitching a quiz to a magazine, read as many recent issues as possible. If you can find quizzes they've run, pay attention to the format used so you can try to match it. For example, if the quiz was multiple-choice, did they give three possible answers per question or four? Was an answer key provided at the end of the quiz or were individual answers given after each question with supplementary information? Use this research to tailor your own pitch.

If quizzes never seem to appear, it doesn't necessarily mean the magazine doesn't use them. It may just mean that (a) no quizzes have fit into the recent editorial mix, (b) they haven't received a good quiz pitch lately, or (c) both. More important is to see if you can find articles of a similar topic to your quiz so you can reference those in your query. My first query to *Men's Exercise*, though I'd never seen a quiz in the magazine before, was for a multiple-choice piece called "Test Your Fitness IQ." They loved it, and have since assigned me several others.

Who Do I Contact?

Call the magazine and say "Hi, I'm interested in pitching a quiz idea to the magazine. Could you please tell me which editor would be the appropriate one to contact?" You might get a direct answer from the receptionist, or, if the magazine is one of many under the umbrella of a parent company, you might get transferred and have to ask the question again. If you can't get an individual name this way, check the magazine's *Writer's Market* listing for a contact name. Failing that, check its masthead and send to the features editor, managing editor, or deputy editor.

GAMES/ACTIVITIES

Related to quizzes are games and activities to which certain magazines allot individual pages or, sometimes, more. Don't imagine such pieces are the exclusive domain of children's magazines—plenty of publications use them. Look no further than *The New York Times Magazine* Sunday crossword, awaited by millions week in and week out, or the recent spate of sudoku pages that have so many subway riders in their grip.

Readers enjoy these pages; games and activities allow them to become interactive participants in the magazine. The best part is that, if you can come up with something that fills a need for the magazine and strikes a chord with readers, you might end up with a column that sticks around.

Games and activities aren't just for kids. Think of how many people make it their weekly mission to complete *The New York Times Magazine* Sunday crossword.

Get This Gig: Games/Activities

Where Do I Start?

Research various magazines and put yourself in the shoes of one of its readers. What kind of fare would you find fun and engaging after flipping through the articles? A puzzle? Brainteaser? Something using pictures? Be creative. Don't be constrained by what you've seen before. The more original an idea you can bring to the table, the better your odds of winning space. No matter the magazine, base your brainstorming on what kind of game or activity you think would suit it rather than how open you assume it would be to the idea. Magazines change format, structure, and content all the time; none remain static. As I write this, for example, the venerable *National Geographic* is poised to debut a crossword puzzle as its newest back-page feature.

Who Do I Contact?

Send your idea to the features editor if one exists. If not, contact the deputy editor or managing editor.

Exercise Patience

Knowing when to conduct a follow-up is the great tightrope act of a writer's existence. We all like to picture an editor breathlessly reading our manuscript and then grabbing the phone to tell us how life-altering an experience it was. Things work a bit more slowly, of course. In fact, the more positive the reaction to your story, the more likely it will be passed around to several editors before a final decision is reached. Difficult though it is to keep anxiousness at bay, especially when every fiber of your being is telling you to send a brief follow-up, it is crucial to exercise patience.

Magazines and publishing houses indicate average response times because they know how much volume they deal with. Sending a follow-up before that response time has elapsed sends the message that you don't do your homework, you don't respect the process, or you consider yourself more important than other writers. These aren't messages you want to send. As writers, we often exhort one another to persevere, but that's something most writers bring to the table naturally. It's the other side of the coin—patience—that can sometimes make the bigger difference. As Tom Petty says, the waiting is the hardest part. But it can also prove the most valuable.

FACTS AND FIGURES

Today more than ever—with attention spans growing ever shorter and schedules becoming ever more crammed—people love when a magazine serves up tidbits and factoids, little morsels of information that entertain, enlighten, or educate. Quick-hit facts and figures often show up near the front of a magazine, providing subtle enhancement of that issue's theme or context.

Facts and figures assignments, though often small, can serve as excellent credits. I once wrote a 1,250-word article for *Golf Magazine* on golf courses located at the farthest cardinal points on the globe. When putting the issue together, the editors decided my piece would work best as a full-page global map with only the names, locations, and contact information of each course included as copy. Though hardly what I'd originally envisioned, it became one of my favorite tear sheets.

10 FACTS AND FIGURES	Think about the different subjects a certain magazine covers. Then see what kind of statistics related to those subjects you can research and relay that the magazine's readers might find interesting, amusing, or surprising.

Get This Gig: Facts and Figures

Where Do I Start?

Call the magazine's offices and ask if you can get an editorial calendar. Knowing what topics are going to be on the editors' minds for the next several months might spark you to come up with some related facts and figures pitches—and that would show them that you do your legwork.

Who Do I Contact?

If your idea concerns a particular section of the magazine that has an individual editor—say, the fashion section of a women's magazine—contact that editor directly. If not, the managing editor or deputy editor is a safe bet.

Someone Who Could Hold A CONVERSATION WITH STEPHEN HAWKING GIVES HER TOP THREE SUBMISSION TIPS

Hildy Silverman, publisher, *Space and Time*

1. **Know your target audience.** If you're asked to write an article on innovations in fertility treatments, your results should look much different depending on whether the readers are doctors or couples battling infertility. Editors want to know that you not only

understand the material but also can tailor it to the appropriate audience.

2. **Proofread!** This may seem obvious, but a surprising number of writers shoot articles or stories off to editors without properly reviewing their grammar, punctuation, and spelling—the basics. This is especially true when it comes to electronic submissions. One misspelled word may seem like a minor issue, but it can mean the difference between you landing an assignment or it going to that other writer who bothered to take the extra step.
3. **Read the magazine.** Whether you want to pitch a nonfiction article or a fictional story to a magazine, read at least two issues first. Everything you need to know about the audience, style, and preferred subject matter is available between the covers.

ADVICE COLUMNS

Dear Abby kicked it off, and countless others have taken up the mantle. Doctors, lawyers, financial advisers, psychologists, wedding planners, former coaches, Jimmy the Bartender—they and many, many others dole out advice on a regular basis through the pages of a great variety of magazines. For editors, these columns provide reliable content month in and month out. For writers, they can be terrific ongoing gigs that boost both income and profile.

11 ADVICE COLUMNS	What are you an expert in? And what's on readers' minds today? Once you find a topic whose answer is yes on both counts, you've got a potential pitch.

Get This Gig: Advice Columns

Where Do I Start?

Begin by asking yourself what you're an expert in. It doesn't have to be a traditional profession. People don't want only legal, tax, or real estate advice. Off the top of my head, I can think of a pediatrician who has a column about kids' health, a tobacconist who has a column about cigars and pipes, a music producer with a regular installment involving the indie scene, and a fitness instructor with a regular feature about exercise regimens. What specialized topic can you speak to, and on what grounds? Once you have an answer (or more than one) to this question, start thinking about what kind of magazine might be a fit for both the topic and your voice. Then sit down and start crafting the query.

Who Do I Contact?

If you're pitching a regular column, get in touch with the features editor; if a single piece, try the executive editor or managing editor.

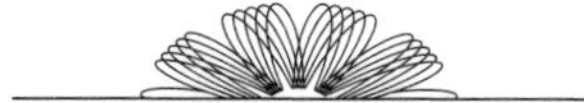

A Veteran Freelancer
BOILS IT ALL DOWN TO 50 WORDS

Alyson Mead, freelancer, Los Angeles, California

Never forget that you're there to serve the editor, and therefore, the reader. They're not there to serve you, your portfolio, or your bottom line. Many writers forget that, to their detriment. Learn to serve the needs of others with pride, not attitude. You are helping them solve a problem.

ARTICLES FOR COMPANY PUBLICATIONS

In my mailbox today is a copy of *The Costco Connection*, a magazine sent by Costco to its members each month. The magazine is filled with stories spun around products the company sells, from a yarn about the ABCs of kayaking to another about portable solar generators.

Now, while we're all aware that *The Costco Connection* is actually a thinly veiled attempt to get you to come to the store and drop a few hundred bucks on things like twelve-packs of canned chickpeas, it's nonetheless a great example of the kind of company publication requiring freelancer expertise. It's clear *The Costco Connection* is not done on a whim—or a shoestring. Glancing at the masthead I see it warrants an editor, editorial director, managing editor, online editor, multiple associate editors and assistant editors, plus—most relevant for you—a dozen different freelance contributors. Costco needs writers to write its stories, as do numerous other companies who have begun to print and/or post their own regular publications as a way of, ahem, keeping in touch with their customers.

12 ARTICLES FOR COMPANY PUBLICATIONS	Numerous companies have begun to produce their own publications as a way of highlighting their products or services to existing and potential customers. And they need writers to write their stories.

Get This Gig: Articles for Company Publications

Where Do I Start?

First, keep all the magazines you get from companies through the mail. I count over half a dozen such magazines I receive these days, including the aforementioned *The Costco Connection,* plus publications from my phone company, my cable provider, Air Miles, The Home Depot, and the parent company of the brokerage firm that manages my investments. I'm not talking about catalogs; I'm talking about real magazines with articles. Flip through the pages of all those you receive and see what kinds of stories they publish. Ask yourself if you can research and deliver similar articles. You'll probably find that the answer is, in several cases, yes.

Next, whenever you're walking through a store, keep your eyes open for a publication sitting at the front counter. More companies produce magazines than you think. If it's free, take one and conduct the same research as described above. If it isn't free, go home and see if it's available online. If it isn't, you may want to go back to the store and invest in a copy in order to do your homework properly.

Who Do I Contact?

If it's a magazine, it has a masthead—that's where you go. Most of the time there will be a single editor, or perhaps two—that's who you target.

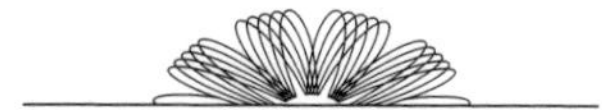

You Don't Know UNTIL YOU TRY

A while ago I wanted to do a roundtable interview with the heads of the top five publishing houses in New York City. At first I assumed it was impossible. But I had nothing to lose, so I called the offices directly, got to the assistants, and asked. Guess how many of the publishing heads accepted? Five. The editor of *Novel & Short Story Writer's Market* was so ecstatic she even gave me a few bucks to take them out to lunch. I flew to New York, did the roundtable, and turned in the piece. In the end, I didn't make any money off it because the amount I was paid equaled the airfare to New York, which I paid out of my own pocket. Why did I do it? Because, as a writer, you must be willing to invest in yourself to build your career.

Two vital things happened as a result of my roundtable with the publishing heads. First, I made important connections—you can't put a price on that. Second, I boosted my reputation. The following year, when the editors at *Writer's Market* wanted someone to do a roundtable with three prominent new novelists, they came to me. The contacting editor told me this is what had been said inside the walls of the conference room: "Give it to I.J. He can get anyone." I'd achieved a perception distinct from the other writers in their stable based on a bit of gutsiness and, more important, the willingness to bite the short-term financial bullet in deference to the long-term opportunities that might result. That kind of risk-taking has paid off for me over and over. The lesson here is disarmingly simple: Sometimes, all you have to do is ask.

TRAVEL ARTICLES

When it comes to travel writing, well, the world is your oyster. Travel pieces are evergreen in literally hundreds of magazines around the world so that their readers can learn about everywhere *else* in the world. Everyone wants to write travel pieces, largely due to a somewhat distorted perception of glamorous assignments requiring them to jet off to exotic locales, sip margaritas, and send home 750 words every few weeks. It doesn't work quite like that, at least not all the time. First, not all locales are glamorous. Second, travel budgets aren't always big. Third, it can often take a lot of research, time, and fact-checking to come up with even a short piece. But travel writing is still lots of fun, always interesting, and great for the resume.

Your upcoming winter vacation to Florida, for example, might be conducive to queries about golf in the region for a golf magazine, traveling with kids for a parenting magazine, Miami restaurant trends for an in-flight magazine, and a snowbird's diary of a Florida trip for one of the local magazines in the area you're traveling to.

Get This Gig: Travel Articles

Where Do I Start?

Go to your local bookstore and start taking magazines off the shelves. Flip through them all, zeroing in on the article synopses contained in the first few pages. There you'll learn whether travel pieces are part of the magazine's directive. For those that do feature such pieces, read them, or at least browse them, so you can appreciate how they're put together. Some are written essay-style, some are broken up by lots of headings. Some focus on setting, some on people. Some are done in first person, some third. Some provide broad travelogues of entire cities, others focus on highly specific aspects of the geography or culture.

Next, think about where you've been and where you're heading next. Your pitch to a magazine's travel editor needs to be couched in reality, whether it's about a place you've recently visited or one that's on your upcoming calendar. Don't e-mail an editor saying, "I'm a freelance writer with numerous credits, and I've always wanted to see the Maldives. I'd be happy to write you a piece on this fabulous destination." However, this might work as a start: "I'm a freelance writer with numerous regional and national magazine credits. Next month I'll be spending two weeks in the Maldives, the smallest Asian country, the country with the lowest high point in the world, and a place of incredible beauty that only recently has begun to make a blip on the radar screens of most international travelers."

Who Do I Contact?

The majority of magazines with travel columns will have specific editors assigned to them. Check the masthead first for a travel editor. If you don't see one, don't send indiscriminately; call the magazine's offices and ask the receptionist the name of the editor who accepts travel queries.

A Picture Is Worth …
WELL, THAT DEPENDS

When sending a travel query, always let the editor know if you have, or plan to have, accompanying photos. Editors are normally happy to pay extra for photos as long as they meet a minimum standard of quality and resolution. Sometimes, offering photos with the piece can make the difference between yes and no.

JOURNAL/DIARY PIECES

There's a reason teenage girls guard their journals with their lives: The writing they contain is straightforward, unadorned, and irresistibly frank. That's why, as an article format, journal and diary pieces tend to work well, too—they allow a writer's voice to be the main feature of the story without anything else getting in the way. The story still has to be about something, but to a great extent the reader engages with the piece based on his trust and enjoyment of the voice relating it. I sold "Diary of a Pool Meltdown" to *Lindy's Baseball* not because I was the first person whose fantasy baseball team had tanked spectacularly but because the editor connected with my voice. The clearest evidence I have for this is that after I e-mailed him the initial pitch he phoned me directly to ask for some elaboration. I knew he wasn't calling to decide whether he liked the idea; he was calling to hear how I actually talked, since that's what he knew would probably come through in the journal-format piece I was proposing. It all worked out—taking at least some of the edge off that miserable fantasy season.

Journal/diary-style format can serve stories of almost any type, but you need to sell the editor on both the idea *and* the voice.

Get This Gig: Journal/Diary Pieces

Where Do I Start?

Don't look at any magazines. Research this from the inside out—that is, start by brainstorming around your own experience, *then* think about what kind of magazine a journal story of yours might suit. If you're a parent of four, maybe a diary of your Disneyland vacation with all the kids would prove funny and relatable to readers of parenting magazines. Maybe, as a member of Doctors Without Borders, your journal-style account of working in the African bush would be tempting to the editors of medical or inspirational magazines. Maybe *Esquire* would be interested in excerpts from the diary you kept during your one-month foray into being a private investigator. Once you've written down one or two areas in which you think your journal/diary-style voice would be authentic, of interest, and timely, start researching magazines that would fit these areas.

Who Do I Contact?

Send your query to the features editor if the magazine lists one. If not, go for the managing editor or executive editor.

RATINGS/REVIEWS

There's nothing people trust more than a straight-up word from someone else, as long as that person knows what he's talking about. Knowing this, many magazines publish articles that function almost as creative public service announcements—they provide factual information usable to some group. From the book and album reviews you find in *People*

to a piece rating the top gardening tools on the market, there are places for this type of article rendered in many different ways and covering a great variety of topics.

When writing reviews, aim for balance. If you're too harsh, editors might think you have an axe to grind. Too flattering, and they might think you can't see both sides.

Get This Gig: Ratings/Reviews

Where Do I Start?

Examine plenty of different magazines and note which ones contain rating/review-type articles. Then start noodling queries based on what interests you, what you know, or, if the two happen to converge, both.

Who Do I Contact?

Some magazines will list a reviews editor on the masthead. If you don't see one, contact the features editor, managing editor, or executive editor, or call the magazine directly and ask for the name of the editor who handles such articles.

 RECOMMENDATION PIECES

Service pieces provide information. Rating/review pieces evaluate something. Then there is another, more innocent animal, the recommendation piece, which encourages people to do something, get something, or go somewhere, and attempts to justify that encouragement.

I recently did an article called "5 Stags for Today's Groom," which, based on the suggestion that the days of the traditional drink-and-gawk bachelor party are going by the wayside, offered five alternatives for today's more open-minded groom, including golf weekends and paintball tournaments. That's an example of a recommendation piece.

16

RECOMMENDATION PIECES

A recommendation piece is an endorsement for something. A good recommendation query doesn't focus on why *you* enjoyed something; it explains how that something would benefit the magazine's readers.

Get This Gig: Recommendation Pieces

Where Do I Start?

Select five magazines at random from the shelf in your local bookstore. For each one, take fifteen minutes to brainstorm a recommendation piece that would seem to fit within the publication's editorial parameters. For a fishing magazine, maybe it's an article suggesting why certain lures are better than others. For a fitness glossy, perhaps you have an innovative new stretching-and-cool-down regimen that allows for 10 percent more workout. The sky's the limit.

Who Do I Contact?

For each query you come up with, check the mastheads of the magazines you're targeting. Some of them will have editors of particular sections to which your idea belongs. When this matching occurs, contact the individual section editors. If not, send to the managing editor or deputy editor.

NEWSPAPERS

If you want evidence that the printed word isn't going away anytime soon, go to your local Starbucks. Turn 180 degrees after purchasing your Frappuccino and you're likely to be standing in front of a neatly kept rack of newspapers, there for your reading pleasure as you sip and linger.

There's a reason Starbucks carries newspapers: The two go together. Just as so many people are unswervingly devoted to their morning cup of java, an equal number just don't feel right until they have their morning paper. Is it because they don't feel they can function properly without being up on the day's news? Not really. It's because newspapers provide a constant element in their lives, a comfortable habit that also happens to let them know what's going on in the world.

Newspapers are the mainstays of the publishing world. Their earliest incarnations were in ancient Rome, when Julius Caesar would have bulletins carved and posted in public places; then progressed to China, where they were written on silk and read by government officials; then to Venice, where for the low, low price of one gazetta you could get all the political, military, and economic news of the day.

Modern newspapers came into their own at the beginning of the seventeenth century with the switch from woodblock print to movable type. (Thank you, Gutenberg.) The first modern newspaper is usually said to be the *Relation aller Fürnemmen und gedenckwürdigen Historien*, published in 1605 in Strassburg, Germany. In the American colonies,

Benjamin Harris was the first publisher of a newspaper, *Publick Occurrences Both Forreign and Domestick* (I know, catchy name), even though the government squashed it after one edition. Of course, the governor did allow *The Boston News-Letter* to be published regularly starting in 1704, so it isn't as though they were completely paranoid. Soon weekly papers started sprouting up in New York and Philadelphia. The *Pennsylvania Evening Post* became the first American daily in 1783, and newspapers have fed our continuous appetite for news ever since.

Newspapers rarely take a day off, and guess what—those stories you're reading in today's paper need to be replaced by new ones tomorrow, and those need to be replaced the day after that. The largest and most unremitting need for words—new words every day, on new topics, seen from new angles—is in those black-and-white column inches you see tucked comfortably under people's arms every morning.

Because of their constancy and exposure, newspapers have proven an excellent springboard for countless writers. Though their rates are lower than those paid by magazines, the volume of writing newspapers require is many times that of magazines. You might hear other writers bemoan newspapers' paltry rates. Ignore those writers; they're short-changing themselves. Say a magazine assigns you two 1,500-word pieces per year and pays you a dollar per word, for a total of $3,000. At the same time, your local newspaper offers you a weekly 500-word column at thirty-five cents a word. That's $175 per column, or $9,100 for the year. Suddenly the per-word rate doesn't seem so terrible, does it?

The Landscape

At last count there were ... let's see, carry the one ... somewhere in the neighborhood of two thousand different newspapers in North America. I'm pretty confident no one has ever calculated the total number of articles that appear in all of these newspapers collectively day in and day out, but let's just agree it's a boatload.

Unlike magazines, which tend to open and close more often than subway doors, newspapers stick around. Most cities and towns have a regular newspaper. Most countries have multiple papers catering to different audiences. Here in Canada there are three national dailies: *The*

Toronto Star, *The Globe and Mail*, and the *National Post*. All have a large, constant readership, and many people read more than one of them every morning. In Toronto alone we have a dozen different papers in half a dozen different languages, from *Canadatürk* to *El Popular*. That's a lot of stories, which means a lot of freelance opportunities.

Newspaper writing rates hover around twenty-five to thirty-five cents a word these days, with some as low as ten cents and some as high as fifty. Rates are determined by several factors, including the size and reach of the paper, your credentials, and the type of piece you're assigned. As I said, try not to dwell too much on per-word rates. Bylines are more important. After all, when you query an editor, she's going to ask for a list of your recent credits, not what you were paid for your last assignment.

The Future OF NEWSPAPERS

Can anyone predict the future of newspapers? Well, yes and no. In North America, newspapers in their traditional format are facing major challenges because of the Internet, skyrocketing newsprint prices, declining circulation, and slumping ad sales. In other parts of the world, thanks to cheap printing costs and growing middle classes becoming more literate, newspapers are on the upswing. India, for example, has nearly as many newspapers as all of North America.

No one knows if the unstoppable forces of change are going to make the customary look of newspapers obsolete. Either way, from a freelancer's perspective, *it doesn't matter*. We as a society have grown accustomed to getting our news, and we aren't about to just abandon that habit. People are going to demand to know about the stories going on around them in some form, whether it's via a daily broadsheet or a streaming media file. And those stories will need to be written by writers, plain and simple. So don't spend your valuable time fretting about whether newspapers are going to look the same twenty years from now as they do today. Just keep your finger on the pulse, be willing to adapt, and keep looking for great story ideas.

OP-ED PIECES

Literally "opinion editorials," op-ed pieces express a view about a certain topic, person, or event. Regular articles, typically written in third person, present a story as part of a broader context or explain both sides of a particular issue and let the reader decide where she stands. Op-ed pieces are distinct because they offer a specific stance on a given issue and are usually written in first person.

The parameters for op-ed pieces are usually wide open as long as (a) you're writing about something relevant and timely, and (b) you aren't offering an opinion too strongly at odds with the paper's general stance or writing in a voice that too jarringly contrasts its customary tone. Don't submit a strongly worded piece about the evil of abortion, for example, to your city's left-wing daily—it ain't gonna fly.

17
OP-ED PIECES

Op-eds are opinion pieces—they express the writer's point of view about a certain subject. Before you submit an op-ed piece to a newspaper, get familiar with its general tone and stance to make sure the piece fits.

Get This Gig: Op-Ed Pieces

Where Do I Start?

Op-ed pieces can be about literally anything, but they do need to touch on something pertinent, and current, in order to have a chance at seeing print. A piece about the impact Jackie Robinson had on baseball may be well written, but the odds on it getting published are a lot better during one of the major anniversary years of Robinson's debut. An essay on the Rwandan genocide of 1994 may be insightful and enlightening, but unless placed within current context, it will probably remain in limbo. Read several op-ed pieces over the course of a week or two to get a feel for what's being printed in your local rags. Then find a timely, relevant topic that inspires you, and start writing.

Who Do I Contact?

Op-ed pieces are usually found in the newspaper's generic or catch-all section, like Life or Viewpoint. Start by considering the specific topic you're writing about. Is it a piece outlining suggestions for better United Nations decision-making? You need to contact the editor of the World or International section. A reflection on a recently deceased music icon? Your target should be the Entertainment editor, or the closest thing to it. If you can't quite figure out where your piece belongs, phone the paper, ask for Editorial, and tell them you have an op-ed piece you'd like to submit but you're not sure which editor accepts them. They'll ask you what the story is about. Have a clear, no-more-than-ten-second answer ready, and they'll let you know whose inbox is the appropriate one.

COLUMNS

It might surprise you just how many regular columns there are in your local newspaper. Flip through and you'll see what I mean. Some of the people writing those columns were awarded them after maintaining a solid track record of reliable contribution; some earned them on the strength of great credentials or a large profile; some simply offered expertise no one else could. Regular columns carry a certain amount of stature and offer benefits like, sometimes, having your black-and-white thumbnail photo run every week for millions to admire. Feature columnists are also assumed to be top-drawer writers, so readers are often fiercely loyal to their work.

Scoring a regular column isn't easy, because (a) regular installments don't turn over that often, (b) columnists themselves tend to keep their columns until they leave the paper, change jobs, or die, and (c) little room is allotted to "new" columns. But it's not impossible. No, columns don't turn over every day, but they do come and go with enough regularity that, if you stay on the ball, you'll eventually find yourself in the right place at the right time. Also, while columnists do stick around until they leave, change jobs, or die, all three events do occur. Finally, though new columns don't crop up as often as, say, celebrity scandals, they do appear now and then, because what's important to readers is always changing. Most papers, for example, have long had columns concerning subjects like money, business, sports, gossip, and relationship advice, but a number have recently added columns on the environment and technology. You just need patience, persistence, and a long-term perspective.

18
COLUMNS

Scoring a regular column may not be easy, but it's far from impossible. Ask yourself one question: What can I talk about with confidence, expertise, humor, and insight? Pitch that subject and yourself as an authority on it.

Get This Gig: Columns

Where Do I Start?

Pick up your local paper. I don't mean your national newspaper distributed locally; I mean your *local* paper, the one printed only in your town, district, or neighborhood.

Do you have expertise in a particular area? Publishers and editors always have to fill column inches, so it's worth asking. What can you offer that people want to know? Maybe you're an expert on consumer culture, or new media, or small business marketing. Your main advantage as a freelancer is that the world changes more rapidly today than ever before. That creates more frequent opportunities to break in, because newspapers are always looking for new people to write columns on topics that satisfy the collective appetite.

Who Do I Contact?

Once you've determined what kind of column you can write and have crafted your pitch, call the paper and ask the receptionist two things:

who to send your query to and how. A growing majority of editors do things almost wholly by e-mail, but some still prefer old-school methods, and those editors genuinely appreciate when freelancers take the time to find out.

NEWS STORIES

News stories are the peanut butter and jelly sandwiches of the newspaper business—simple, reliable, and easy going down. They have to be that way, because they need to be written fast and delivered faster. They let readers know what's been happening in their town or country or world for the past twenty-four hours or seven days. Most of the space in a given newspaper is reserved for news stories, which is why a paper's nerve center is called the newsroom, and why the paper itself is called a *news*paper.

News stories embody a newspaper's primary reason for existence: to make us aware of the things happening around us.

Get This Gig: News Stories

Where Do I Start?

Most news stories will be covered by the newspaper's permanent reporters, but that doesn't mean you can't slip in with the right story at the right time. What special ins do you have, and to what areas? Maybe the person who organized the big social rally on the weekend is a former high school chum who has refused contact with reporters but might open up to you. Perhaps you've written extensively about ecological issues, making you an ideal candidate to deliver a report on the efforts to save the local moraine, forest, wetland, or sand dunes. Stay patient and keep your eyes and ears open. Things will come up, and your job is to act on them—fast.

Who Do I Contact?

As soon as you're ready with the idea for the story, take a few minutes to craft and rehearse your pitch—you should be able to deliver it in less than ten seconds—and then call the newsroom. You don't have to speak slowly, since a newsroom is one of the most feverish places in the known universe, but do be clear and concise, and be prepared to repeat yourself in case you're passed to a different editor. The best thing about pitching news stories is that, even if you don't get the response you want, at least you'll never have to wait for it.

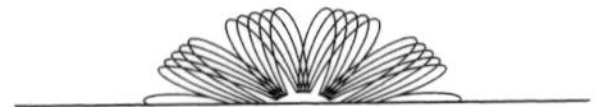

A Veteran Newspaper Journalist SPELLS OUT HIS FIVE GOLDEN RULES

Don Vaughan, Raleigh, North Carolina

1. **The job of a freelance writer is to make an editor's job as easy as possible.** This means maintaining an exceptionally high level of professionalism—which isn't difficult to do. Pitch ideas with the editor's market in mind. Respect your deadline, word count, and other demands. Deliver clean, well-edited copy. Keep in mind that most editors are too busy to clean up a lazy writer's poorly edited work and almost certainly will not give a lazy writer a second opportunity.

2. **Keep your editor informed throughout the writing process.** In talking with editors, the complaint I hear most frequently is that writers don't listen to instructions or don't keep their editors in the loop when researching and writing. Editors loathe surprises, so if a problem arises, let your editor know immediately, not two days past your deadline. Failure to do so can have a ripple effect with serious consequences.

3. **Always remember that the relationship you have with an editor is a business relationship.** You have a

product to sell, and your editor is in need of that product. It's okay, even encouraged, to be friendly with an editor, but keep in mind that an editor is not your friend. He doesn't care about your cat or how your day went. All that matters is that you do your job well.

4. **There are certain questions that should be asked every time you get an assignment: What is the fee, and when will I get paid?** What's the deadline? What's the word count? What rights are being bought? Do you want the article as proposed? This last question is vital. It's important that you and your editor are on the same page regarding the tone, content, and direction of the article you're being asked to write.

5. **Stand up for yourself, and don't be afraid to negotiate a better deal when you feel it's warranted.** Generally speaking, editors have two fees—the one they offer you when they make an assignment, and the larger fee they're authorized to offer if you simply ask for it. Explain the complexity of the article, the amount of work involved, or the tight deadline. Most editors understand and are willing to offer more. The same goes for provisions within a contract, such as rights. Almost everything is negotiable.

HUMAN INTEREST STORIES

The centenarian who somehow squirreled away half a million dollars during her lifetime and is giving it all to the town library; the local teenager who started a charity for hungry kids in Africa that has grown to become one of the largest of its kind; the assistant manager at the car dealership who also happens to be a world-class competitive hot dog eater. They all provide wonderful newspaper fodder. Why? Because we're fascinated with each other—always have been, always will be. Or, to steal a line from the stage production of E.L. Doctorow's *Ragtime*, "People love to see what people do."

Human interest stories are the warm and fuzzy flipside to the tragic blazes, grisly murders, political shenanigans, and corporate scandals that unfortunately populate the front page on a daily basis, and therefore are part of the bread and butter that keeps newspapers chugging along. And editors are grateful when an appealing human interest story crosses their desk because such stories add a welcome contrast of texture, authenticity, and warmth to the cold, hard facts that provide the grist for most stories.

20 HUMAN INTEREST STORIES

Human interest stories have to meet only two criteria: They have to be about humans, and they have to be interesting.

Get This Gig: Human Interest Stories

Where Do I Start?

Anywhere and everywhere. Interesting stories are around every corner. Sometimes you don't even have to go as far as looking around the corner because they're right in front of you.

The number-one technique for finding good human interest stories is asking questions, all the time. If you're at a dinner party and someone mentions a friend who rode his bike to South America and back to raise money for multiple sclerosis research, don't let him off the hook. Ask for more details. Contact the friend and get the fleshed-out version of the story to see if it might be something an editor would want. Do this whenever you get wind of anything that might seem of even moderate interest. You never know what's there until you dig a little deeper.

Who Do I Contact?

Human interest stories don't belong to any one section of the paper; they tend to be peppered throughout depending on the topic and the particular angle the writer has chosen. So you need to research the specific journal you're targeting. Read it for a week (if it's a daily—a month if it's a weekly, a few months if it's a monthly) to see what types of human interest stories they publish and where such stories land. Then call the paper's offices to get contact information for the appropriate editor, and off you go.

EVENT REPORTING

Interesting things are happening all the time—in your neighborhood, in your town, in your state, in your country, in the world. In outer space. Within atoms. *Everywhere.* And there isn't a newspaper editor who wants to be the one to have missed an important scoop that another paper has snagged. It makes editors' jobs immensely easier when a writer comes to them having found out about, say, the two hundredth anniversary of the first fire hall in town instead of them having to go through the dual step of (a) unearthing the story in the first place, and (b) finding someone to write it.

21 EVENT REPORTING	Interesting things are happening all the time, everywhere. Deliver well-written stories on noteworthy occasions or occurrences and you'll quickly gain pet status with editors.

Get This Gig: Event Reporting

Where Do I Start?

A good first step is to head to your local library or chamber of commerce and read about the history of your town. From this you'll no doubt find a number of upcoming milestones or anniversaries to write about. An editor will be impressed by your research, and by writing about potentially obscure events you'll start to establish a reputation as a good newshound.

You can never begin this process too early. In 2006 I found out about one of the most remarkable things that had ever occurred on the PGA Tour: four different players scoring holes-in-one on the same hole, on the same day, within two hours of one another, at the 1989 U.S. Open. The odds of it happening had been estimated at 1.87 quadrillion to one. I made a note in my calendar that year to start querying editors in 2008 about writing the story for its twentieth anniversary in 2009. I carried the note over every month for two years, finally queried in late 2008, and got the assignment.

Who Do I Contact?

A single event can be approached from several angles and therefore can be slotted into a variety of sections in the paper. Say there's an international kite-flying competition being held in your city. You could interview one of the champion kite flyers, or write about the process of designing and building kites, or about the history of kites, or you could recommend it as a weekend family outing, or you could bake it into a personal essay about your own memories of flying kites with your older brother. Decide what perspective you think best serves the piece, write a great query making clear that perspective, then check out the newspaper you're querying and it will probably be obvious to you which section editor to get in touch with.

BEAT REPORTING

A "beat" is a specific something covered exclusively by the same reporter all the time. It might be the local high school football team, the mayor's office, or the new-restaurant scene. Securing a beat can help your freelance career in two ways: First, it builds your profile by having your writing read by the same, often large, audience consistently; and second, it's steady work.

22 BEAT REPORTING	Read your local newspapers and ask yourself one question: What might people want to know about on a regular basis that isn't being covered now?

Get This Gig: Beat Reporting

Where Do I Start?

Beats are hierarchical. Start at the bottom rung of the ladder and work your way up. If your ultimate aim, for example, is to cover the office of the president of the United States, begin by approaching your regional paper and asking if they need someone to cover a local government official's office. The work may seem uninspiring at first—think of poor Kate Hudson in *How to Lose a Guy in 10 Days*, having to write a fluff column instead of the global-issue-solving pieces she so desperately wishes to pen—but you must think of it as a stepping stone on your way up. Take a page from Dave Barry, who writes about his early days writing for the *Daily Local News* of West Chester, Pennsylvania:

> *I spent many hours sitting through municipal meetings wherein local officials would discuss issues such as sewage, zoning, street signs, sewage, budgets, storm drains, and of course sewage—the issues that, although not glamorous, are the "meat and potatoes" of local journalizzzzzzz*
>
> *Sorry. I nodded off there, as I often did in the meetings I covered. But this did not prevent me from writing massive, fact-filled stories that ran in the Daily Local News, usually under real "grabber" headlines like: BOARD AIRS SEWAGE PLAN.*

Like I said, every journalist has to earn his stripes. If there is a specific subject you *know* you want to write about, start immediately by trying to get a beat in that area, in any newspaper you can, whether it's your national daily or a community circular. Don't worry about how much or how little it pays. Once again, it's crucial to maintain a long-term, big-picture outlook. Your goal is to accumulate experience and credits for your résumé.

Who Do I Contact?

Once you have a tight, specific query ready, do whatever you can to make inroads with the relevant editor at the paper you're targeting. Remember that newspaper editors are often swamped, so follow up diligently but professionally.

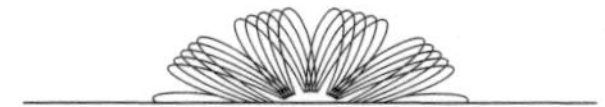

Three Newspaper Editors ANSWER SIX BURNING QUESTIONS

Q *How nutty is your typical day?*

Tom Maloney, sports editor, *The Globe and Mail*: It would take a thousand words to give you a full description. Let's just say on most days eleven hours seemingly spin by in the span of a normal job's three.

Tom Arthur, senior editor, *The Tampa Tribune*: Between swine flu, a mass murder up the road, and the local legislature arguing over gambling, there's always plenty to sort out.

Johanna Love, features, arts, and entertainment editor, *Jackson Hole News & Guide*: I get back to my desk after the weekend and have 150 new e-mails, a dozen phone messages, and a large stack of paper to get through. It takes me all week to sort through it. Scratch that—I never actually make it through.

Q *How fast do you normally respond to queries?*

Tom Maloney: Usually the same day, otherwise they get buried in an e-mail avalanche.

Tom Arthur: I make it a practice not to let them sit for more than a day.

Johanna Love: If it's a great query and I'm interested, I write back right away. If I'm not interested or not convinced the piece is a good fit, I might delete it, or I might let it sit for a while before reading it again.

Q *Name three differences between a good query and a bad one.*

Tom Maloney: First, length: In fewer than 100 words, I'll either say go, no, or ask for more details. Beyond 100 words, I'm losing interest quickly. Second, tone: I need to feel that the publication is going to be the worse without this story and that you in particular have the credentials to execute it to a high standard. Third, pertinence: *The Globe and Mail* covers a limited range of sports and appeals to a generally definable demographic. When I'm offered a story that doesn't pertain to our coverage universe or to our readership, it's easy to assume the writer doesn't read our section. We will often venture outside the coverage corridor for an offbeat feature, but the subject needs to be relevant to the readership. Allow me to add a fourth comment: E-mail makes perfect sense, but I receive one hundred messages a day easy. An old-fashioned stamped envelope with a nicely typed letter arrives maybe once every two weeks.

Tom Arthur: The queries I tend to like have a local hook, have potential for good visuals, and quote more than one source.

Johanna Love: A good query is spell-checked, concise, and makes me want to read the story. A bad query has my name spelled wrong, uses all lower-case letters, and lacks specifics. Bottom line: Convince me that you have a good concept, you possess sufficient experience to write it well, and you have done a similar thing before and pulled it off for somebody else.

Q *How far ahead of time should someone pitch you a time- or event-specific story?*

Tom Maloney: The sooner the better. Get on the radar screen. And I don't mind reminders.

Tom Arthur: Preferably a week.

Johanna Love: Three weeks.

Q *What's the best part of your job?*

Tom Maloney: Every day there's something different, and when we're about to break a story or publish an enterprising feature that will give fodder to the bloggers and sports radio or TV stations for days, it's that much sweeter.

Tom Arthur: Same answer as number one.

Johanna Love: Reading entertaining stories.

Q *What's the most challenging part?*

Tom Maloney: Keeping everyone happy and motivated.

Tom Arthur: Same answer as number one.

Johanna Love: Getting every detail right. That means I have to be on the ball, and I have to hire writers who are on the ball, too.

INTERVIEWS/PROFILES

As a society, we love celebrity—even minor celebrity. We love to create celebrities, and we love to tear them down. We love to give people their fifteen minutes in the spotlight and then move on to the next flavor of the month. Our fickle culture works to the advantage of freelancers, since readers never tire of getting the inside scoop on who's doing what.

Maybe an A-list star is blowing into town for a couple of weeks to shoot a new movie. Maybe a business owner on your block is spearheading a new green initiative to cut carbon emissions throughout your city. Both scenarios are newsworthy, and in both cases the person at the center of the story is its highlight. Why not see if the papers would like an exclusive interview?

23
INTERVIEWS/ PROFILES

Don't think of celebrities as the only people worth interviewing. People are doing interesting things around you all the time.

Get This Gig: Interviews/Profiles

Where Do I Start?

Start your steady climb up the food chain by finding people in your own city doing remarkable things and pitching interviews or profiles of those people to local publications. Early in my career I spent a year or so doing an interview each month with a different former high school classmate for my local community bulletin. I made a pittance, but the experience was invaluable—it gave me both interview credits and tear sheets that showed I could put together an interview piece. In college I edited a weekly newsletter that included a profile of one of my fellow on-campus undergrads. I don't know if anyone ever read the thing, but again, writing those profiles gave me experience I could cite and also taught me how to tell stories about different people from different backgrounds.

Before pitching the interview/profile, do three things: First, get confirmation that your subject is willing to be interviewed; second, determine how soon he can be available; and third, gather enough material on your subject to craft a substantial pitch.

Who Do I Contact?

The editor you contact will be determined by what kind of interview/ profile you're writing. Are you interviewing the star high school athlete in your area? For that, you'll e-mail the sports editor. Is it a profile of a big-name business tycoon? E-mail the business editor. If it isn't obvious who to contact, or if your story seems to overlap more than one section of the paper, it's best to call the main newsroom, offer a brief description of your story, and ask. Again, newspaper people are by and large extremely helpful, even though they're extremely pressed for time.

REVIEWS

Yes, the Internet has changed the habits of readers, but the first place most people still go to find out whether they should see that new film is their local paper. Same goes for books and music. The trusted local newspaper reviewer awarding the new Will Smith blockbuster three out of four stars is all the endorsement most people need. On the other side of the coin, if that same reviewer pans the latest John Grisham novel, a large percentage of readers are going to heed the non-recommendation and bypass the book. Reviewers wield considerable power and influence, which for most of them is a serious perk of their jobs.

Movies, books, and music are three of the four main areas that garner newspaper reviews. The other is restaurants, though often those reviews end up in a different section—the former three usually in a section called Entertainment or something similar, the latter usually in a section called Food or Living or What's On or Your City or something of the sort. Editors love writers who can write a satisfying, balanced restaurant review with a bit of flair—kind of like a good meal.

24 REVIEWS	Newspapers often have regular reviewers for movies, books, music, and restaurants. But those reviewers often leave, and someone has to fill their shoes.

Get This Gig: Reviews

Where Do I Start?

Decide which kind of reviewing appeals to you most. Then write a review in that area, heeding the word count provided in the guidelines of the newspapers you're targeting. Do it quickly, because the window is small—someone else might be writing a review of the same thing and wanting to submit it to the same editor.

Keep in mind the paper's typical tone. You want to write in your own unique voice and style, but you also want to be cautious not to diverge from the attitude the newspaper has spent years establishing.

Who Do I Contact?

Call the newspaper and simply ask for the name and contact information for whichever editor is appropriate—the books editor, films editor, music editor, or restaurant/food editor—then, submit!

COMIC STRIPS

As a kid, I read only two sections of the paper: Sports—every day—and the gloriously colorful foldout Comics section that came in the Saturday edition. While downing my two ritual bowls of Raisin Bran, I'd read every single strip, from *The Family Circus* to *Beetle Bailey*, *Calvin and Hobbes* to *The Far Side*—sometimes twice. They were special, those comics pages. It wasn't as though I needed a break from the heavy news, since, as I said, I didn't even acknowledge the existence of any daily content beyond box scores, but the comics still carried a certain magic and warmth. They were funny, like *Adam*, and serious, like *For Better or For Worse*. They were clever, cheeky, offbeat, and provocative, and they conveyed entire stories with the use of a few panels and some captions, endearing them to me even more. I was never able to draw worth a lick, so I never aspired to create comic strips of my own, but I say with confidence that comic strips, as much as any other form, inspired me to write.

Most every newspaper includes a comic strip. Sometimes it's a single-panel strip plugged into the Entertainment section. Sometimes it's *Dilbert*, featured in Business. Frequently it's a political strip, like *Doonesbury*. The incongruity served up by a comic strip is a tool editors can use to great effect to balance the otherwise serious content of the paper, like giving your spouse a spontaneous tickle in the middle of a serious discussion.

Remember that comic strip editors look for the same things story editors look for: believable characters in entertaining situations.

Get This Gig: Comic Strips

Where Do I Start?

Ask yourself two questions: Can I draw, and can I write? You need to be able to do at least one of the two to author a comic strip. A number of comic strips are done by author-illustrator teams, so if you can only write, you need to find someone who can draw, and if you can only draw, you need to find someone who can write.

The next step is to create samples of your comic strip. Try it out on some people whose reactions you trust to know if it stacks up against those you read in today's weeklies. Once you feel it's sufficiently focused and tight, prepare three sample strips to submit.

Who Do I Contact?

Every paper you can. It's difficult to know which newspapers have a desire for new comic strips, so submit to as many as you'd like. Make sure you include your local papers, which will in all likelihood provide the best opportunity for you to get some exposure. Your ultimate goal is for the strip to be picked up and syndicated in papers all over the country. But first things first.

Who you contact will depend on the size of the paper. If there's a features editor listed, he is the one to get in touch with. If you don't see anyone on the masthead with that title, try the managing editor. And if there's no one with *that* title—which will commonly be the case with smaller local papers—contact the plain old editor.

POLITICAL CARTOONS

Similar to comic strips but more specifically placed are the cartoons poking fun at our political representatives, often showing them as dull-witted caricatures exhibiting a whole suite of unenviable traits including dishonesty, greed, foolishness, and venality—which in many cases isn't off the mark, but I digress. We all love political cartoons because, well, we all have politicians we'd like to hang by the thumbnails. If you can reflect that collective loathing in a funny, topical way, let the papers know!

26 POLITICAL CARTOONS	To draw political cartoons, you don't have to be a political expert. But you do need to reflect the collective political mood in an entertaining way.

Get This Gig: Political Cartoons

Where Do I Start?

It's a matter of knowing what the standard is for the paper you read. Find the political cartoon in your paper of choice and study the drawing style, the humor, the general viewpoint it seems to represent (this might come across subtly, but it's important), and the kinds of themes it uses to make its point. Then, think of ways to put your own stamp on things—perhaps your own particular style of caricature or captions that convey a slightly different brand of humor.

Once you've established what you feel is a distinct, consistent style, create a few sample panels for submission. Make sure they address current, or least recent, issues.

Who Do I Contact?

The person to contact is the editor of the section in which the cartoon appears. This will be different for every paper.

PERSONAL ESSAYS

The first newspaper credit I ever earned was for a brief essay about trying desperately to distract myself from wanting to call my ex-girlfriend following our third breakup. Six months later I was at a local authors' festival promoting my short story collection, and several people, seeing my name, made reference to the essay that had appeared in the newspaper half a year earlier. Personal essays can be nicely conspicuous items in newspapers for the same reason they aren't part of the umbrella of traditional journalism. To be frank, I find it hard to distinguish one piece of political reporting from the next, but I remember a great many poignant, inspiring, heartwarming, heartrending, funny, or eye-opening personal pieces that have appeared in newsprint.

27 PERSONAL ESSAYS

Personal essays can be about anything at all. Before sending in your work, make sure your piece conforms not only to the paper's submission guidelines but also to its general tenor.

Get This Gig: Personal Essays

Where Do I Start?

Some newspapers have a dedicated essay page; some sprinkle them here and there on a more or less sporadic basis. Do your homework by collecting several issues of the paper you're pursuing and checking the spots where essays most frequently appear.

Who Do I Contact?

Sometimes the information you need is provided right at the bottom of the column itself. Sometimes it's contained in a recorded message on the paper's main phone or on its Web site.

If you can't get the information in one of these ways, do it the old-fashioned way: Just call and ask. As I said, people who work at newspapers are typically accommodating but also tremendously time-starved, so don't expect to engage in a conversation. Ask for the information you need, take it down, repeat it back once to make sure you've got it right, say thanks, and hang up. If the person on the other end truly has no clue how to help you, get the name of the features editor. Any of the "softer" stories that aren't news—essays, interviews, etc.—fall generally into the category of features.

A Hardy Newspaper Veteran GIVES IT TO YOU STRAIGHT

John E. Phillips, Birmingham, Alabama

1. **Nobody cares what you *want* to write.** If you want to make money as a writer, write what an editor will buy.
2. **Be a problem solver, not a writer.** If you solve problems for editors, you'll get all the work you want.
3. **Find out what type of article an editor will buy before you write the query.**
4. **The best way to get steady work is to get face time with editors.**
5. **Write a query so interesting that an editor will have to ask for the manuscript to find out what happens.**
6. **Send out thousands of queries each year.** This is a numbers game, so the more queries you send out, the more editors you'll get to know and the more work you'll receive.

CONTESTS

While newspaper-run contests—typically for short stories or poetry—are not frequent, they are a great place to potentially get your writing read by thousands, or sometimes millions, of people. These contests may offer winners a decent amount of cash, entry into a coveted writing program, or valuable street cred. No matter the tangible prize, what a contest win gets you is a sparkling credit to cite on every subsequent submission you make. Keep your eyes out for contests, and, unless the entry fees are prohibitive, submit to every one of them you can.

Contest wins, almost-wins, or honorable mentions are nice ways to distinguish yourself in submission cover letters. Get a list of newspaper contests from your copy of *Writer's Market* and force yourself to enter at least half a dozen of them.

Get This Gig: Contests

Where Do I Start?

Check the Contests section in your copy of *Writer's Market*. Check *Novel & Short Story Writer's Market*, too. From those two publications you'll find contests run by major newspapers. Then Google "newspapers + contests" and expand your list. Finally, list all of the local papers in your area, then call them and ask what kind of contests they run, if any, what the deadlines are, and where you can find submission guidelines. That way you don't get waylaid by a contest deadline that's only days away and have to whip together something you know isn't as good as you could have done if you'd only had more time. In this business, the more tactical you can be, the more places you'll see your writing published.

Who Do I Contact?

All contests have specific guidelines that include information about who to send to and how to send.

HOW-TOS

Need to know how to clean your barbecue for spring? Organize your garage more efficiently? Dry a bouquet of flowers in a practical-yet-creative way? That's the kind of information other people want, too, and you could be the writer who helps them get it. Don't think of how-to's as the newspaper's nuts-and-bolts, meat-and-potatoes, black-and-white, and therefore noncreative, stories. They can be as thoughtful, amusing, interesting, evocative, or thought-provoking as you'd like.

Often it's the characters in a how-to piece that make the story come to life, and the more obscure the matter you're describing, the more intriguing the characters frequently are. That is, if you're explaining how to start a hedge fund, those who provide source input might not be the most enthralling cast of characters, no offense to hedge fund managers intended. But maybe you're writing instead about glass-blowing. Or how to weave a carpet. Or the proper way to diffuse a bomb. Those kinds of topics would no doubt give you some interesting people to chat with, and some interesting material with which to write a highly informative and highly entertaining piece.

29 HOW-TOS	One strategic way to think about how-to articles is by season. In October, for example, start thinking about things people might want to know how to do for spring.

Get This Gig: How-Tos

Where Do I Start?

Answering this question is like answering the question, "Where do you get your ideas?" The correct response is, of course, *everywhere*. You don't have to be told to keep your antennae up for interesting topics, because one of the very things that makes you a writer is your compulsive need to find out more about everything that passes by your eyes or ears.

That said, you do need to demonstrate to editors the skill of separating wheat from chaff—discerning what people want to know about, in contrast with things that are of mild interest but not ultimately meaty enough to warrant column inches. Sometimes this will come down to instinct, but it also depends on your ability to ask good questions, report the answers accurately, and mix all that useful information into a readable, interesting story.

Who Do I Contact?

Since how-to pieces are typically unplanned—that is, not part of the regular slate of articles—send your idea to the features editor.

 EXPOSÉS

Also sometimes referred to broadly as investigative journalism, exposés, through in-depth reporting, hard-hitting research, and the use of multiple sources, reveal untoward dealings in some form—corrupt business practices, political skeletons, celebrities behaving badly, that sort of thing. Exposés typically elicit layered reactions. They can brand you as a writer who knows how to ferret out the truth and provide a valuable public service, and at the same time they can alienate you or cast you as one of "those" writers in the business who punish bad people for doing bad things. Not that people shouldn't be punished for doing bad things. But be careful.

If you are going to pursue exposé writing, there are a few things to keep in mind. First, don't ever count on a single source. Second, don't ever file a story unless you're 100 percent certain of its veracity. And third, even if you're expressing a clear opinion about the story, be sure to present both sides. It's okay to come across as passionate or opinionated about a certain issue as long as you have your facts straight.

30 EXPOSÉS	If you're going to tackle exposés, observe three important rules. First, use multiple sources. Second, make sure you've got all your facts right. Third, give both sides of the story.

Get This Gig: Exposés

Where Do I Start?

Bad stuff is, unfortunately, going on all the time, probably not too far from you, or possibly right under your proverbial nose. Of course, tips about unseemly behavior aren't going to just fall in your lap; you have to go out and get them. One way is to hook up with a detective agency. They exist—you probably just don't know about them because you've never thought to contact one before. You might also call your local police precinct and ask to talk to some of the officers about cases they're investigating. Same goes for law firms—there are plenty of those around. Sure, there will be many things people won't want to, or can't, talk about, but if you make a practice of being politely nosy—curious but not meddling, inquisitive but not intrusive—you'd be surprised what you can find out.

Who Do I Contact?

If and when you do get that plum story about someone doing something unbecoming, keep it under wraps until you know the story is valid and you've done exhaustive research. The last thing you want is to become known as a false whistle-blower. Once you've got your ducks in a row, contact the newsroom, inform them, and ask to meet with someone in confidence. Don't tip your hand or reveal any confidential information until you've been given a signed contract for the story.

SEASONAL ARTICLES

Seasonal articles refer not just to the literal seasons but also articles tied to any specific period or habitual observance. An article about the origin of Christmas wreaths is seasonal. So is a story about the cherry blossom trees given by the Japanese to the Americans and their dream-like annual blooms. Or a piece recommending the safest toboggans for your kids to go zipping down hills.

Editors appreciate being queried about seasonal topics far in advance so they can plan ahead. So brainstorm away—and plan at least six months ahead.

31 SEASONAL ARTICLES	When brainstorming seasonally based articles, the most important factor is timing. What's too far in advance to pitch an editor a seasonal story? Most say there's no such thing.

Get This Gig: Seasonal Articles

Where Do I Start?

There are always new things to write about, or new slants to present, with regard to the seasons, the holidays, or other traditional ceremonies and celebrations. Google a list of different holidays and start brainstorming ideas around them. Write an essay about the secret recipe for Passover latkes passed down through five generations of your family. Do a story on the endearingly zany people who participate in polar bear swims every winter. Sneak off to Edgar Allan Poe's grave on his birthday and wait until the middle of the night to see who might show up and what they might offer to him as tribute. The possibilities are limitless.

Who Do I Contact?

As a default you can submit to the features editor, who will redirect you if the story is more appropriate for someone else on the editorial team.

SERVICE ARTICLES

If you're querying an editor with a piece that will inform people about a certain consumer product or service, that's a service article. The article will be fairly straightforward. Though it will be written in your unique voice, of course, it will also need to deliver on a few specific criteria: introducing the product or service, outlining its key attributes, and demonstrating why you're writing about it rather than, say, a competing product or service in the same area. An alternative approach might be to compare the top two brands of a certain product, or the most popular half-dozen, or maybe to discuss the chief pros and cons of something that's just hit the market. However you frame it, the dual purpose of a service article is to make readers aware of a certain something and help them make an informed decision about it.

32 SERVICE ARTICLES	Though it will be written in your distinct voice, remember that a service article's main purpose is to inform, not entertain.

Get This Gig: Service Articles

Where Do I Start?

Everyone writes best about the things that interest them, so consider the kinds of products or services you find particularly neat—nanotechnology? Workout gear? Organic produce?—and start doing some research in that area. As you proceed, remember that you're doing the research on behalf of potential consumers, so ask all the questions to which you yourself would want answers. Try to get access to primary sources, like the team leader who oversaw the design of the product. Your story will be the better for it.

Who Do I Contact?

If the newspaper you're targeting has special sections—like a Technology section in the Saturday edition—and one of those sections applies to the product or service you're writing about, contact the section editor. Otherwise, contact the features editor.

TRAVEL PIECES

We all share an insatiable curiosity about the rest of the world, which is why travel articles show up in just about every newspaper you can find. Such pieces are meant to communicate important details about a particular destination—what to do, where to stay, must-sees, hidden gems—while at the same time conveying something of its culture and spirit. When you're querying about a travel story, be clear about whether you've already been to the place so you could write the story tomorrow, or will be going at some future date, in which case the editor would have to plan for it. Also, let the editor know if photos are available with the story—that can sometimes swing the decision.

Writing "I'll be visiting Wichita next month. Like a story on it?" isn't likely to win you an assignment. Instead say, "Next month I'll be visiting Wichita, recently ranked by *Money* as ninth on the list of the ten best U.S. big cities in which to live," and you'll get bites on a regular basis.

Get This Gig: Travel Pieces

Where Do I Start?

Ideally, by traveling—although you don't necessarily need to visit a place to write about it. I once did a story for *Canadian Geographic* about the northernmost golf tournament in the world, which takes place near the Arctic Circle. I wasn't able to actually visit the town of Ulukhaktok, where the tournament takes place, but I did spend a great deal of time tracking down the people who organized the event, those who'd played in it before, and others who could provide substance to the story.

Who Do I Contact?

The majority of newspapers have a travel editor, whose contact information should be listed either in the paper itself or on its Web site. Failing that, call the offices and ask.

LITERARY OUTLETS

Look up the word literary and you discover a two-part equation: "fictional," "mythical," and "legendary" make up the first part; "erudite," "scholarly," and "literate" make up the second. I believe the dual explanation captures exactly what we all aim for in our most important, most personal writing: magic mingled with intelligence; the real blended with the fantastic; and unique, unforgettable characters rendered in relatable, familiar ways.

It's this transcendent chemical reaction literary publications seek, too. They embody our highest collective writing aspirations and demonstrate the limitless ways in which words can be put together to produce wondrous results. Great literature moves us as nothing else can. It produces feelings we don't get from any other form of art. And the journals that exist to publish such writing are the vital conduits allowing us that possibility again and again.

The Landscape

Of all the questions writers ask, the most common may be, "Is there still a place to publish serious literature?" The answer is, as always, yes. Generations of readers have shown that fine writing will always have an audience, and dedicated publishers have shown that it will always have a place to be read. Literary journals and periodicals maintain an exclusive, irreplaceable presence in the writing world because the people who run them are devoted to the ongoing search for great manuscripts and nothing else.

Most literary journals are university-run endeavors, labors of love, or both. They're run largely on blood, sweat, and tears and survive mostly because of the efforts of the small staffs who maintain them out of a pure love of good writing. Pay rates are typically on the low side, with many offering nothing more than contributor copies. Some literary markets pay healthy rates in line with magazines, and a few pay quite handsomely.

Of course, your chief purpose for getting published in literary outlets shouldn't be money, anyway. It should be to accumulate credits and build your profile. You may not get a big check from having your short story published, but keep in mind that literary journals are the places book editors and publishers tend to look in the search for new literary talent. Having one or two of them as credits in your resume goes a long way.

As such, competition for space in literary journals and periodicals can be intense, but believe editors when they tell you a rejection slip isn't a rejection of your work, just a statement that it doesn't happen to fit their particular needs at that time. Every editor I know has to turn down many pieces worthy of publication every year based strictly on space. So don't stop submitting. Ever.

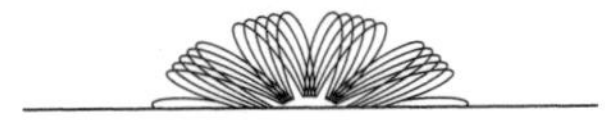

Strategic Searching

You'll see numerous spots in this book in which I advise you to use the subject index in your copy of *Writer's Market* to find publications suitable to the market you're investigating. Don't forget the critical supplemental tool that is *Writer's Market's* online site, www.writersmarket.com. There you'll find reams of information to assist in your searches. Or maybe the Web site is the primary tool and the print version secondary. These days, who knows? Anyway, my point is: Use both!

SHORT STORIES

People love stories; they always have. Why did our ancestors feel compelled to depict their buffalo hunts on cave walls? Because we, as human beings, want a record of our existence and our perceptions of the world. It's why all forms of art attract us. We love impressionist paintings because they show us what we already see, but in an unexpected form. We love sculpture because it presents us to ourselves in a slightly different but thoroughly familiar fashion. And we love stories because we recognize ourselves, and those around us, as the characters in them.

The history of short literary fiction is long, rich, and varied. Tennessee Williams wrote gorgeous stories. Mark Twain wrote hilarious ones. Edgar Allan Poe wrote a bunch that still make me shiver in my boots. Why do so many authors who hit it big with novels feel the need to publish short story collections? Because short stories are probably the literary tool they started out with, and the one for which they still have the deepest affection.

Short stories still offer the best way not only for writers to sharpen their teeth but also for those same writers to have their talent showcased. Look at the current edition of *Novel & Short Story Writer's Market* and you'll find venerable journals like *The North American Review*, going strong since 1815, new kids on the block like *Notre Dame Review*, which came on the scene only in 1995, and every type of short story outlet in between. There will always be a place for stories because a good short story is like a glittering gem—precious, beautiful, and lasting.

34 SHORT STORIES	Golden rule number one: Always maintain a steady flow of story submissions. Golden rule number two: Always maintain a detailed log of what you've sent where.

Get This Gig: Short Stories

Where Do I Start?

Researching short story markets is, for most writers, an enjoyable exercise because there are so many. Crack open your copy of *Writer's Market* or *Novel & Short Story Writer's Market* and start listing story markets. Don't make it a single list, however, or you're liable to feel overwhelmed in short order. Create a few different lists according to certain criteria, like story length, pay rates, specific genre needs, and response time. This will enable you to be more considerate in your submitting and will also help you keep track of what's been sent, and where.

Whether you're sending your manuscript to a small-circulation periodical or a big consumer magazine, make sure it's polished internally and externally. That means make sure the story itself is as good as you think it can be, and also make sure it's packaged exactly as requested. If they want it via snail mail, don't e-mail it. If they want one-inch margins, don't use inch-and-a-quarter because you think it makes the pagination more appealing. They want to see your creativity *in the story*: Everything else is just to show that you can play by the rules.

Who Do I Contact?

Look in your copy of *Novel & Short Story Writer's Market* or in the masthead of the journal itself for the name of the person who reviews short story manuscripts. Typically this person will have the title fiction editor, story editor, or literary editor, though depending on the size of the publication their role might be less specific—editor or senior editor, for example.

The Editors of Two August Literary Magazines **ANSWER THREE IMPORTANT QUESTIONS**

Q *What, for you, makes a manuscript sing?*

Linda Landrigan, editor, *Alfred Hitchcock's Mystery Magazine*: I look for writing that is tight, yet has a musicality and rhythm. I like to see a fully imagined world of the story, with strong characters and logical plotting that is evenly paced. I like to be surprised by a story, but I don't like surprise endings; like most mystery readers I enjoy the process of arriving at a solution as much as the final unveiling of the truth.

Janet Hutchings, editor, *Ellery Queen's Mystery Magazine*: It is so many different things. There are different kinds of appealing stories: those I buy because of a clever plot, those that have an unforgettable voice, those with characters I can't shake, those with special atmosphere ... it goes on.

Q *Do you react the same way to a great story now as when you first started?*

Linda Landrigan: I think I have a deeper appreciation and love for the art of the short story now.

Janet Hutchings: I'm still thrilled by a great story when I come across it, and that will never change.

Q *How much of a manuscript do you have to read before you know if it's a winner?*

Linda Landrigan: I know how difficult it is for writers, so to be as fair as possible I try to read the entire story, unless it's obviously wrong for us.

Janet Hutchings: You can usually tell within the first sentence or two whether the author has control. Then you'll either be taken in by the actual story or not. Of course, even if the author has the knack for storytelling, there may still be problems. And as Linda said, some stories, no matter how good they are, simply aren't appropriate for the magazine.

SHORT SHORTS

You've probably heard a zillion times to vary the length of your sentences so your story doesn't stagnate. That's true, you should. The shake-it-up principle applies in many other areas of life, too. If you do the same workout over and over, your fitness level plateaus. Go to the same restaurant with your significant other every week and the relationship starts to feel stale. Read nothing but the sports section of the newspaper and you box yourself in conversationally and socially.

Editors, too, heed this principle when considering their story lineups. As you read through an issue of your favorite literary journal, notice the variation in narrative length. That's no accident. One of the ways in which this variation is sometimes achieved is through the inclusion of short shorts (also called microfiction, flash fiction, or sudden fiction): stories of no more than 1,000 words, or, depending on the publication, a few hundred. Short shorts aren't meant to be snapshots, vignettes, or excerpts suggestive of something larger; they're complete, fully realized stories that merely happen to occupy less space. And they aren't just poor second cousins to traditional-length short stories. *Writer's Digest*'s Short Short Story Competition, for example, or *Grain*'s Short Grain writing contest, offer great ways to get noticed.

As haiku are to longer poetry, short shorts can be to longer stories—unexpected pearls that take hardly any time to read yet are nearly impossible to forget.

Get This Gig: Short Shorts

Where Do I Start?

Do a Google search for short shorts, flash fiction, or microfiction to get a taste for its structure and cadence. Visit www.wingedhalo.com and www.kennesawreview.org, the Web sites of *Flash Me Magazine* and *Kennesaw Review*, online magazines that publish flash fiction. Also, get your hands on copies of print publications that run short shorts, like *The Cream City Review* and *Isotope*. Then give it a whirl. Don't get down on yourself if, like children's writing, you find it harder than anticipated. When you finally create a short short that works, you'll feel like you've fashioned a diamond out of thin air.

Who Do I Contact?

Scour *Novel & Short Story Writer's Market* for two types of markets: those that clearly indicate they consider short shorts, and those that indicate length needs as low as 500 words. Either type is fair game.

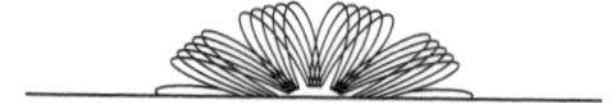

Three Prominent Literary Editors ANSWER THE QUESTION, "WHY ARE STORIES IMPORTANT?"

Ben Metcalf, literary editor, *Harper's Magazine*: It's one of the things we can offer the aliens as justification for not destroying us. You look at a well-made short story like you look at a beautiful painting or wonderful piece of music. If a human being did this, the entire race can't be that bad.

C. Michael Curtis, senior editor, *The Atlantic*: I think we tell stories because they teach us how to be. They give us examples of people making choices and discovering the consequences of those choices. Before we were ever able to write, storytelling provided explanations for things.

Adrienne Miller, literary editor, *Esquire*: Fiction is essential for our emotional survival. Telling a good story is the most beautiful thing any person can do.

POETRY

Unfortunately, poet-philosopher no longer counts as a job title—Aristotle sure did have it good—but that doesn't mean the world has lost its appetite for poetry. Quite the opposite, in fact. The busier we get and the faster the wheels of industry and technology spin, the more we appreciate a beautiful piece of verse that can carry us momentarily away. Poetry has the same magic-dust effect on us it always has. It just tends to be harder for most of us to find time to read it.

Nonetheless, the market for poetry remains healthy and diverse. *Poet's Market* lists no fewer than one thousand potential poetry markets, from *Crab Orchard Review* to *The New Yorker*, including over sixty poetry-related contests and awards. Yes, poetry is alive and well, and just as much a salve for our souls as it has ever been.

36
POETRY

Contrary to popular belief, it isn't any harder to publish poetry today than in the past. It's *always* been a challenge to publish poetry. But the markets are out there, and they're hungry for great poems.

Get This Gig: Poetry

Where Do I Start?

Read a lot of poetry and write a lot of poetry. Like a painting or sculpture, there is no purely objective way to decide whether a poem is poor, adequate, or phenomenal, but ask ten people what they think of Wordsworth's "Daffodils" and you'll probably get a consistent response.

Once you've got some poems you think might be publishable, consult your copies of *Writer's Market* and *Poet's Market*. Match your poem—its format, length, and theme—with the criteria indicated by the literary outlets listed. Some avoid rhyme; others favor sonnets; others publish only haiku. Pay attention also to which publications ask you to submit no more than a single poem and which invite groups of three or five poems at a time.

Who Do I Contact?

Certain publications have a poetry editor. If you don't see one, simply use the contact name provided in the listing. If there's no contact name listed, call and get one.

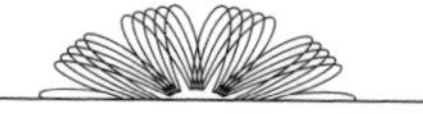

Performance Poetry

Most anywhere, there's a community of poets, or readers of poetry, who gather regularly to soak in the beauty of verse. Often these groups hold poetry slams, open mike evenings, or special readings. Sometimes prizes are given out. I used to receive a monthly phone call from a wonderfully boozed-up fellow named Christian inviting me to a poetry slam a few evenings later. I could seldom make out the particulars because he always sounded like he'd just been hit by a wrecking ball, but a couple of times I detected enough information to make it to one of his events. Christian's evenings would be organized in a fun way—everyone paid a three-dollar cover to share their poetry with the crowd, who, at the end, would vote for the top three, and those people would split the money 60-30-10. One of my poems, "Accidentally Considering My Penis," even took top prize at one of Christian's poetry slams—though I still haven't been able to get the darn thing published. Too niche, I guess.

PERSONAL ESSAYS

The personal essay, that self-contained piece of reflection, meditation, or inspiration, has always had an important place in literature. Essays are like a bridge between stories and poetry, combining the two forms into one. A well-spun essay has the power to transport us briefly, like a poem, but can also deliver the satisfaction of narrative, like a story. Essays appear in literary publications large and small, new and established, local and national.

37
PERSONAL ESSAYS

A personal essay should be written spontaneously but submitted tactically. Pick up a copy of *The Sun*, *Tin House*, and *The Georgia Review*. Would you send the same essay to all three publications?

Get This Gig: Personal Essays

Where Do I Start?

First, write about what moves you, *then* figure out where to send it. While essay subject matter can of course be timely, there's no such thing as an "essay trend" or a particular type of essay being sought by editors at a given time. Boundaries for personal essays hardly exist, so just make it real and make it good.

Place yourself in the shoes of an editor or a reader and work that story over as pitilessly as you would a piece of fiction. Remember that just because a given event was meaningful to you doesn't automatically make it meaningful to a reader. People tend to resist editing their essays because they don't want to remove material about things that actually happened to them. Even if you delete some of the prose, the experience still occurred. Remember the elements of strong storytelling technique: focus, pace, and precision.

Who Do I Contact?

Refer to your copy of *Writer's Market* and make a note of all the essay markets. (There are tons!) Most of the time you won't see anything like an essay editor for a given publication, so get in touch with the contact individual they give you. If you want, you can always call them and ask them for the name of the editor who accepts essays.

Never Stop When You
THINK IT'S GREAT

Whenever you read through a manuscript and pronounce it ready for the mail, place it aside and come back to it a few days later. At that point commit to making it just a little better, even if that improvement amounts to tightening a single paragraph or replacing one almost-right word with a more exact one. You owe it to yourself to set your own standards high.

Once a manuscript is done, get it out there and don't worry if another edit occurs to you three days later. There is scarcely a writer in existence who looks back on a manuscript and believes it's perfect. Or, to quote Anthony Burgess, "You don't say, 'I've done it!' You come, with a horrible desperation, to realize that this will do."

WRITING-INSTRUCTION PIECES

No doubt you have a lot you could share about writing—the craft, the business, the writing life. And no doubt other writers, established, aspiring, and not sure whether they're established or still aspiring, would be interested in those thoughts. Sandwiched among the stories, poems, and essays in most literary journals and periodicals are articles about the world of writing and publishing. Such pieces tend to be highly valued by the readers of these publications, since the readers are, of course, writers, and all of them realize that writing is an ongoing journey and an endless progression. None of us, after all, has learned everything there is to know.

38 WRITING-INSTRUCTION PIECES	What particular writing tricks have you gathered over time? List a bunch of them and see which ones might lend themselves to a full article.

Get This Gig: Writing-Instruction Pieces

Where Do I Start?

Check out publications like *Byline* and *Writers' Journal* to see the kinds of instruction pieces they use amid the more traditional literary substance. Then think about what your strengths are when it comes to writing. Take one of these topics and craft a query. Remember that the purpose of an instruction piece is to help people write better or publish more, so in your query, don't just describe the proposed article; explain why readers of the publication will be better for having read it.

Who Do I Contact?

The person listed as the contact in *Novel & Short Story Writer's Market* is often the story editor or fiction editor—not the individual to whom you want to send an instruction piece. If the main editor is listed, send it to that individual. If not, call to get her name.

INTERVIEWS

Though interviews and profiles aren't the heart and soul of literary publications, they are often important appendages. *The Paris Review*, for example, runs a Writers at Work interview series featuring important contemporary writers discussing their work and the writing craft. Many other literary journals do something similar either on an individual basis or as part of ongoing series.

The question you're naturally asking yourself is, "How do I get access to prominent writers?" The answer is often simpler than you might believe: Ask. I've interviewed quite a number of renowned publishing types. The first was Scott Turow, not long after *Presumed Innocent* had skyrocketed up the best-seller lists. You know how I got to him? Went to his Web site, got a phone number, called his assistant, and asked. It hasn't always been so simple, of course. Frequently I've had to ask more than once, or go through multiple people, or remind them three times that they said yes weeks before. Sometimes it just won't work out, of course. But you can only find out by trying.

39 INTERVIEWS	Never operate under the assumption that you can't get to someone for an interview. Always assume you can until proven wrong.

Get This Gig: Interviews

Where Do I Start?

Find out which publications use interviews by going to the subject index in *Writer's Market*. Then check the listings of each of those publications to see what kinds of interviews they run. Are they straight Q&A or more open-ended profiles? One-on-ones or roundtables? Hard-hitting or soft touch? Focused on up-and-comers or veteran bestsellers? Once your reconnaissance is complete, pick a writer each publication would love an interview with. Then try to get to that writer. Usually you can find an access point via the writer's Web site or through the publisher of his most recent book.

Avoid promising an interview before you know you can get access to the writer. People have done this before, sometimes with success, but it's an awfully risky proposition for one simple reason: Word gets around within publishing circles, and if you tarnish your status with one editor, you might just find that others aren't so quick to assign you things. Be willing to do the grunt work up front and you'll carve out the kind of reputation editors love—as someone resourceful, reliable, and, above all, willing to go the extra mile.

Who Do I Contact?

Interview queries should be sent directly to the publication's main editor or, if there is one, the features editor.

Ten Burning Questions
WITH WILL ALLISON

Will Allison has been around the literary block and back—he's taught creative writing at The Ohio State University, served on the staff of the Community of Writers at Squaw Valley, worked as executive editor of *Story*, editor-at-large for *Zoetrope: All-Story*, and been a freelance editor and writer for more than a decade. His first novel, *What You*

Have Left, was published in 2007 by Free Press. Here, Will shares his thoughts on the writer-editor relationship, the thrill of a great story, and the irrepressible writing bug.

Q *You've been both writer and editor. Which is harder, and why? Does having experienced each side of the coin make you appreciate the other more?*

For me, it's harder to create a fictional world from scratch than to try improving on one that's already on the page. I believe that being a writer makes me a more sympathetic, if no less rigorous, editor. And certainly editing, which involves getting at the DNA of other writers' work, has informed and benefited my own writing.

Q *Give me your top three tips for short story writers trying to get published.*

Number one, read a lot of short stories. Number two, write a lot of short stories. Number three, keep revising those stories. I'm not trying to be glib, but this is what it boils down to—understanding what makes a good story and pushing your own work until it reaches that standard. If those aren't your top priorities, no other tip is going to help you get published.

Q *What is the most challenging part of freelancing?*

Striking the right balance between freelancing and my own writing. It's hard to turn down work, especially in such a hand-to-mouth business, but for me the point of freelancing, as opposed to a more steady and lucrative career, is having the time and flexibility to write what I want to write.

Q *What do you find the most enjoyable or exciting part?*

I get a lot of satisfaction in seeing my work pay off for clients, especially when a writer I've edited gets a story or book published, wins a contest, is accepted to a writing program or conference, etc.

Q *When did you realize you had the writing bug, and what did you do to feed it?*

I first started thinking of myself as a writer in high school, working on the school paper, but I didn't write anything I'm still proud of until many years later. Along the way, I fed the writing bug the only way I know how: by writing and reading a lot.

Q *What are writers' biggest misconceptions about editors?*

That an editor is going to ruin their work, or that their artistic integrity will somehow be compromised as a result of being edited. I'm always surprised at the number of writers I meet—newer writers mostly—who don't want to be edited. I *want* to be edited—edited well, of course, but definitely edited. Nothing has been more valuable to me than the editing I've received from my wife, from my former teachers, and from the book and magazine editors I've had the good fortune to work with.

Q *When you begin a story, are you thinking about specific publications, or are you just trying to write the best story you can and worry later about where it might end up?*

With nonfiction, I almost always have a specific publication in mind, but with fiction, I almost never do. Anyhow, most literary magazines are looking for pretty much the same thing: great stories.

Q *What's most important: plot, character, or dialogue?*

I think the elements of a successful short story are so interrelated that it's impossible to separate them out and hold up one as being more important than another. Everything has to work, and everything has to work together.

Q *What do you tell people who become frustrated at the difficulty of getting published?*

For short story writers, I remind them that a lot of getting published is luck. It's a matter of finding the right editor at the right magazine at the right time. Just because your story gets rejected doesn't mean it's not publishable.

Q *Is the feeling you get as a writer having finished a great story similar to the feeling you get as an editor receiving one?*

One is a sense of accomplishment; the other is a sense of discovery. Though of course discovery is also a big part of writing, and there's a strong sense of accomplishment to be had in editing someone else's story well.

DRAMA

Certain literary publications apportion space for dramatic prose, like excerpts from plays or stories written in play form. For an example (a gut-busting one), read Woody Allen's one-act play "Death," which appeared in his 1975 collection *Without Feathers*. Even if you haven't written this kind of piece before, don't discount it. Imposing dramatic structure on otherwise traditional narrative can make for plenty of interesting and unexpected creative possibilities. And it might just produce the kind of manuscript that stands out from the pack.

40 DRAMA	Though publications rarely specify dramatic pieces among their needs, many are willing to consider them. Even if you don't see it spelled out, don't make assumptions; call and ask the question.

Get This Gig: Drama

Where Do I Start?

You'll notice in your copy of *Novel & Short Story Writer's Market* that many publications indicate no specific need other than "quality writing" or something similar. This vagueness is deliberate; they're keeping themselves open to anything that might turn their fancy, including successful forays into drama. If you aren't sure, call and ask if they consider dramatic pieces such as play excerpts. Also, look in your copy of *Writer's Market* under the section entitled Playwriting, which lists over one hundred markets.

Who Do I Contact?

Most of the time, the main editor is the person you should send dramatic pieces to. If you aren't sure, or if no main contact is listed for the publication, call to get a name.

EXPERIMENTAL PIECES

Writing is fluid, not static, over time. Read the top novels of a century ago and they'll sound considerably different to you from those of today. Editors know this, so they appreciate writers who throw off the chains of convention, push the boundaries, and explore new horizons—as long as those writers do it successfully. Experimental writing, like anything alternative, is risky only insofar as it can stand out for better *or* worse. But by and large, editors are open to attempts at new forms and will give them a fair shake. A few years ago I asked Gordon Van Gelder, editor of *The Magazine of Fantasy & Science Fiction*, whether a story has to follow certain conventions to be publishable. He said this: I stay away from the word "publishable." We ran one story a few years ago that consisted entirely of footnotes. But a common flaw I see is stories that are fragments—pieces in which the feeling or mood is the highest priority, and once that emotion is evoked, the author drops the rest of the story. There's no interest in completing the narrative arc as long as the epiphany is deeply felt. That doesn't often work for me.

In other words, feel free to create new worlds, explore new possibilities, and use language in new ways, but don't just experiment for experiment's sake. The experiment must still be a vehicle for the story.

41 EXPERIMENTAL PIECES	Many writers have found success pushing the envelope of convention. Research properly and submit strategically, and your experiments stand a good chance of finding a home.

Get This Gig: Experimental Pieces

Where Do I Start?

Open your copy of *Novel & Short Story Writer's Market* to the category index and look up Experimental. Then review each of the publications listed to see if you can ascertain whether they might be open to your newfangled literary approach. Sometimes you'll hardly be able to tell, because you'll hardly know how to define your own experiment. If nothing seems to rule out the type of piece you've written, give it a shot.

Who Do I Contact?

The editor. If he isn't listed, go the publication's Web site or call to get the name—and remember to ask for the right spelling.

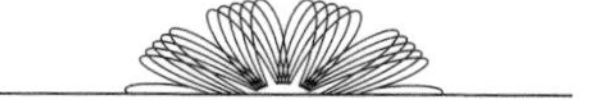

Three Big-Time Writers Answer
ONE VERY IMPORTANT QUESTION

Q *What's better, sex or nailing a sentence?*

David Rosenfelt, author of *Bury the Lead*: I don't think anyone would consider me an expert on either, but I don't know anyone who has a sentence drive.

Raelynn Hillhouse, author of *Rift Zone*: Compare the number of people writing books and the number having sex and you know which is more fun.

Lawrence Block, author of *All the Flowers Are Dying*: I'd say it depends on your audience.

TRANSLATIONS

Publications will often include stories translated from other languages as counterpoint to the English stories that occupy the bulk of their pages. Do you speak in a tongue other than English? Are there writers in that language you admire, or whose work you think might translate in an interesting way? It never occurs to most writers to translate others, but doing so can add an appealing wrinkle to all the other writing skills you offer.

42 TRANSLATIONS	Do you speak multiple languages? Are there writers in other languages you particularly admire? Literary translation is a special skill—one you may be able to put to use.

Get This Gig: Translations

Where Do I Start?

Find authors who write in a language you speak and whose work you enjoy. If you find a particular story by that author that you think might transfer effectively to English, get in touch with the author and make a request to do the translation for the purpose of submitting to an English publication. Be sure to iron out potential payment splits up front in the case of acceptance—for example, you get half for doing the translation and the author gets half for, you know, writing the story in the first place.

Who Do I Contact?

The story editor if there is one, the fiction editor if appropriate (you may be translating nonfiction), or the general editor.

REVIEWS

Freefall Magazine, published out of Calgary, includes reviews under its needs. *Landfall*, from Otago University in New Zealand, seeks reviews of Kiwi books. Both the *South Carolina Review* and *The Southeast Review* list reviews among the types of writing they look for. So, while you're doubtless spending most of your waking hours trying to create your own publishable work, should the mood strike you to provide an opinion about someone else's efforts, go for it.

A good review needs to satisfy three requirements. First, it has to be well written. Second, it has to be timely. Third, it has to be fair. The first shouldn't be a problem, since you're a writer. The second demands only that you contact a publisher ahead of the release date to request a review copy. The third is, for many writers, the most challenging, because, frankly, it's hard to be objective about someone else's success in the area of our own passion—or, as Stephen King put it, once you decide you want to become a writer, "You read everything with grinding envy or weary contempt." Both of these feelings must be put aside when you sit down to properly review others' work. It's okay not to like or recommend a book, but don't get personal or nasty. Stay professional, stay detached, and remind yourself that this review is above all a piece of writing that you are preparing to be submitted to, and considered by, an editor for publication—thus it deserves to be the best piece of writing you can make it.

43
REVIEWS

Journals and periodicals from across the literary spectrum consider it part of their natural responsibility to appraise the writing that's out there, or about to be.

Get This Gig: Reviews

Where Do I Start?

Reviews aren't one of the more obvious or frequent needs listed by most publications, so to find those that do consider them, you might have to examine the listings one by one. If the information is vague or you've seen a review in the publication before even though such a need isn't indicated, call to get confirmation and details.

Who Do I Contact?

Unless you see a reviews editor listed—and most of the time you won't—call the publication's offices and ask for the name of the editor who works with reviews.

CORPORATE WRITING

I hear a lot of writers say they're averse to corporate writing, and I'll be honest with you—I don't get it. Corporate assignments can be fun, stimulating, and rewarding on a number of levels. They come in numerous forms, so they're great for expanding your range and your repertoire. They normally pay well. One assignment frequently leads to others. And more often than not you get the opportunity to work with bright, passionate people who truly appreciate your talent.

I suppose most writers instinctively take umbrage with corporate writing because they feel it isn't *true* writing. Again, I don't get it. When someone asks what defines me as a professional writer, I say this: I know how to tell a story. Sometimes the story is one of my own making—that's fiction. Sometimes the story is someone else's—that's corporate work. But the two aren't mutually exclusive; there's more overlap than one would think. Companies are trying to tell their story, or parts of it, all the time—to customers, prospects, stakeholders, investors, even their own employees. But the people who work at those companies have typically been hired because they're good accountants or good engineers or good assistants or good strategists—not, for the most part, because they're good writers.

Organizations everywhere are sorely in need of those who know how to communicate well on their behalf—in short, those who know how to tell a story. That's you, and you ought to take advantage of the unique ability you've been blessed with. Not everyone has. So don't think of corporate work as a departure from real writing; just consider it a different type of writing. Once you get a taste, you might find you love it for the same reasons you love writing a short story: When you start to put words together in just the right way, that certain magic takes hold, and it is, I'm sure you'll agree, the greatest feeling in the world.

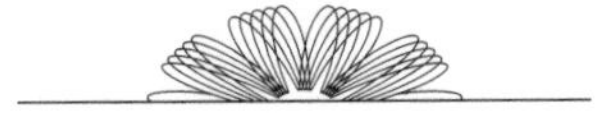

Putting Yourself OUT THERE

If you're just launching your freelance business, there are a few things you need to take care of. At the top of the list is getting business cards and letterhead printed. When you do start to tell people about your practice, the last thing you want is to be stuck without a card to hand over.

The second thing is having your elevator speech at the ready. This is the thirty-second description of your business that provides someone enough information to get a good sense of what you do and also hopefully piques her interest so she contacts you to find out more.

The third thing is letting people know you're in business by sending out an introductory letter and/or e-mail. When I launched my practice, I sent out hundreds of introductory letters—to those I knew, those I didn't know, people, businesses ... just about everyone whose address I could get. I discriminated little in this initial blitz, though naturally with each letter I dropped into the mailbox I became even more nervous that all the money, time, and effort I was expending might lead nowhere.

Then I received a phone call. One of my letters had gone to a high school acquaintance working at a company that manufactured and distributed musical compilations on CD. She had received my letter just as her boss was looking for a writer to help write snappy liner notes. Years later, this company remains one of my biggest corporate clients.

Another of my letters went to an old colleague. He had become the head of an executive degree program at a local university and was preparing to design that year's program brochure, for which a writer was sorely needed. I won the assignment, which led to another three.

The lesson? You never know where work is going to come from. More important, you can't count on finding yourself in the right place at the right time; you have to create the possibility of being there.

The Landscape

Corporate gigs will fall generally into three categories—Big Dogs, Small Fish, and Lone Wolves—each of which offers certain advantages to the astute freelancer.

Big Dogs are large companies with lots of employees, multiple divisions, and, frequently, offices in various locations. Such companies have constant writing needs in the form of memos, presentations, and reports. Though they usually have in-house communications departments, they also have managers and executives who oversee large budgets and sometimes choose to outsource specific needs. Sometimes an executive will come to you to request a minor writing project, like taking a few PowerPoint slides and "making them sound better." The immediate need may seem small, but consider that if you pass this test with flying colors, the same executive is more likely to think of you the next time she has a document in front of her that she senses could be improved.

Because Big Dogs are large operations with multiple layers, heavy politics, and plenty of red tape, they can be harder to crack—but once you're in, they can become serious and steady income sources. Do good work for one department and your name gets passed along to the next. Satisfy the needs of one important decision maker and you might end up doing ten different projects for that same individual. Work well with a project team of half a dozen people on one assignment, and there sit half a dozen individuals from whom you might just get tapped for a big contract down the line.

The best way to approach Big Dogs is with a well-written, professionally presented, one-page letter clearly laying out your credentials and your specific services, including examples. For instance, I offer writing and communications consulting services, so I let prospects know that I'm happy to edit an internal memo, design and implement a comprehensive integrated communications program, or anything in between. Always try to indicate the entire range of what you do without going on too long about it.

Don't send your letter to the communications department. Those are the people who don't want your existence to be known by the people they are, after all, supposed to be serving. And don't send it to the attention of reception or the company's general mailbox. Get the name of a specific high-ranking individual either by visiting the company Web site, checking their annual report (if it's a public company), or simply calling and asking—and then send it to that person directly.

The vast majority of businesses today are Small Fish, successful but modest operations employing fifty people or less. Small Fish can be excellent clients for several reasons. First, they tend to make decisions quickly because there's minimal bureaucracy hindering the process. Second, hard work and good service are truly appreciated because those employed by the company have to work hard to make money and stay in business. Third, the sense of collaboration and partnership can be highly rewarding, since you'll often be dealing with the same one or two people on various assignments.

If you want your existence to be known by Small Fish, get in their faces. Don't simply send them a letter; it's likely to get lost in the shuffle. Employees at Small Fish often carry out multiple duties beyond their specific job descriptions, so they'll have little time to pay attention to any unsolicited letter that crosses their desks, no matter how polished.

Here's what you do instead. First, study the company and its objectives and list a few ways your services might be applied to assist them. Refine those ideas into concrete points. Find out the name of the company president or CEO—John Jingleheimer, let's say. Then, in a crisp professional outfit, walk right into their offices. Tell the receptionist your name and, with a smile, ask if you might speak to Mr. Jingleheimer's assistant about an important matter.

When the assistant comes out, introduce yourself and, again with a smile, briefly mention your services and ask when you might grab ten minutes on Mr. Jingleheimer's calendar for an introductory discussion. The assistant might invite you in on the spot; have your discussion points ready in case that happens. More likely, the assistant will offer you time on another day. Accept it, present her your letter, ask her if she could kindly give it to Mr. Jingleheimer when time permits, and say thanks.

Before you leave, get either the assistant's card directly or get her e-mail address and phone number from the receptionist. Within two days, confirm the appointment. If the assistant calls to cancel at some point prior to the meeting, ask immediately for an alternate time. Keep at this until you get that meeting. Those ten minutes represent an opportunity for you to present yourself and communicate why your services are valuable. This isn't a hard sell, however; it's simply an introductory meeting to let the prez know who you are, what you offer, and a few ways in which your talents might benefit the company given its objectives. There won't likely be the offer of an assignment then and there, but don't be surprised if one comes along sooner than you think.

Lone Wolves, the entrepreneurs and sole proprietors largely responsible for keeping the economy chugging, are constantly overwhelmed because they wear multiple hats—president, bookkeeper, administrative assistant, legal counsel—in order to keep their businesses profitable. On one hand, those in business for themselves are naturally more cautious about where and how they spend their money, so they might devote a seemingly agonizing amount of time to thinking about, say, a $500 contract before pulling the trigger. On the other hand, Lone Wolves eventually embrace the idea of delegating specific needs and are thrilled by a good return on investment.

Translation: While Big Dogs may send a lot of referral work your way from within their own walls, when you do a great one-off assignment for a Lone Wolf, the positive ramifications are threefold. First, you become an immediate preferred vendor—their go-to person, the one they turn to whenever a major writing need comes up. Second, they start to think you should maybe have a look at everything they write or circulate, since, if every time you work on something it comes out sounding better, how could they *not* pass everything by you? So you start to get notes asking you to just "have a look" at this memo or that presentation. A few hours here, a few hours there—it adds up. Finally, the great work you've delivered generates invaluable word of mouth, and the ripple effect from this can continue for years.

Connecting with Lone Wolves is largely a passive exercise; once you send your blitz letter or e-mail, they're more likely to find you than you are them. Referrals will likely come initially from family or friends. Knock every project out of the park, and, as the word-of-mouth ripple begins to expand outward, the Lone Wolves among your clients will become a larger, increasingly diverse group, each one counting on you to help sustain their livelihoods. I don't know about you, but I consider that a pretty special responsibility.

Three Critical BITS OF INFORMATION

Once you blitz the market letting everyone know you're in business, you're going to start getting inquiries, possibly faster than you expect. To keep the momentum going, you'll need to have three crucial pieces of information constantly at hand.

1. **Your rate.** When your work is accepted by newspapers, magazines, or literary journals, you'll have little say about what you're paid. Once you become established, you'll earn a bit of wiggle room when it comes to negotiating rates upward, but only a bit. For the most part, rates are set. But when you write for the corporate market, it's you alone who determines what to quote for a given assignment or project, and this will be based on the hourly rate you determine for yourself. *Writer's Market* lists low, high, and average rates for every type of writing you can think of. Base your hourly rate on this data. When people ask what

you charge, don't be sheepish. Answer quickly and firmly. The more you sound like you believe in the value of your services, the more potential clients will believe it, too.

You'll see under the What Do I Charge? sections that I talk in terms of hours, not dollars. This is because (a) every writer's rate will be different, so it isn't fair to assign a blanket dollar amount to a specific type of project, and (b) within the same type of project there will be different sizes of projects. A presentation might be five slides long or fifty; a speech might be three minutes long or thirty. So when you quote on a project, do it based on a fair assessment of how many hours of your time you think it will require. Don't approach a project thinking "How much money do I want to make off this?" because you'll inevitably skew your own estimates according to a number of factors, including how much money you do or don't have flowing in at a given point. That will lead to inconsistency in your quoting, which clients will come to recognize. But quote according to a true projection of the hours you'll need to do the project and do it well, and clients will come back again and again.

2. **Your contract.** Develop your own standard freelance agreement so you're never in danger of doing a project without having something in writing. (No pun intended.) Companies are often rushed to complete their projects, and the last thing the middle manager assigned to find a writer wants to do is go through the extra step of having to prepare a formal agreement just to allow you to edit his marketing brochure. Send him your own agreement instead, outlining clearly the nature of the project, the expectations on your part, the agreed fee and deadline, and the set number of rounds of revisions before extra time kicks in. This

document doesn't have to be long—mine is barely two pages. The important thing is that you get a signature. You may be reading this and thinking it's a giant pain in the rear end to create a contract every time you get a corporate assignment. Consider this scenario: The manager who's contacted you to write a long marketing piece, along with Web site copy, for a total fee of $3,500 has bolted from his company for a position elsewhere. The marketing piece has been handed off to someone else, and this person doesn't feel that the expense of a writer is worthwhile. If you had only a verbal agreement with the previous person, you've just lost $3,500. If you got it in writing, you've made $3,500.

That's the more elaborate scenario. The much simpler, and more frequent one, involves your having to chase a client for payment. It would be nice if this never happened, but any veteran freelancer can tell you more stories than she'd like about delinquent clients. Without signed agreements, getting them to pay is like trying to précis Hemingway. Get all your corporate assignments in writing and you'll never have to worry.

3. **Your range of services.** When someone asks, "Do you write ___________?" say yes, even if you presume the thing he's referring to may be a form of writing for which you have no inclination. Give it a shot anyway, because there just might be a lot more work hidden behind that first offer. You're a writer, and that means you can (a) write whatever people need written, and (b) enjoy the writing no matter what you're writing about. So when they ask if you write speeches, the answer is yes. Edit annual reports? Yep. Adapt a company profile from print to the Web? Absolutely. Start out by being a bit indiscriminate in the assignments you take. It will help you build a diverse profile and

broad client base so that, as your career progresses, you can pick and choose more often.

PRESENTATIONS

Visit just about any corporate office today and it's a good bet you'll find at least one person cobbling together slides for a PowerPoint presentation. Presentations make the corporate world go round, and virtually every organization welcomes the person who can make them sound good and flow smoothly.

People in business make a lot of common mistakes in their presentations that will prove easy fixes for you—like jamming too much text onto every slide, using punctuation inappropriately at the end of bullet points, and employing different parts of speech to lead off points within the same list (for example, starting the first four bullets with verbs and the last with a noun. Or, as I saw on a bus stop bench ad taken out by a real estate broker last week: "Passionate. Innovative. Experience.").

Executives often find it easy enough to put together impressive individual slides or pages but struggle to find the thread that pulls them all together. I admit to getting a little thrill whenever a client contacts me mired in frustration because she can't figure out (a) what she wants to say in her presentation, (b) how she wants to say it, or (c) both. In general, I take her out of the presenter's shoes and place her in those of the audience. (How much or how little do they know going in? What's the most important message you want them to take away—the bottom line? What part of the content do you think they'll find most powerful, unusual, or surprising?)

Then I ask her to send me all the material she has. Clients, I find, are often reluctant to send along the whole ball of wax because they don't want to bury you with irrelevant information. I prefer the opposite. I want it all, because I never know where the true story, the theme, the anchor, is going to come from, and I've found that, just as often as not, it comes from somewhere the clients didn't expect it to, since they were already too close to it to see the forest for the trees.

Once I've identified what I believe is the thread, I build a proposed storyboard that has as its goal the bottom-line message I asked the client about previously. I also ask the presenter at the outset whether he likes to be highly scripted, hardly scripted, or somewhere in the middle. Then I prepare notes accordingly—in the client's voice, not mine—and try them out on the client. Usually he's relieved and grateful, and also a little pleasurably mystified.

"Great presentations are remembered; weak ones, too. That's why it's always worth recruiting the right person to help nail it."

—George Georghiades, Associate Principal, McKinsey & Company

Get This Gig: Presentations

Where Do I Start?

Ask friends of yours employed by companies if they'd mind giving you copies of presentations that cross their desks. Then practice with those presentations, figuring out where you could improve language, story, structure, and flow. Companies also frequently publish presentations online these days. Do a random Google search of companies in your region, then go to their Web sites and see what you can find.

In your introductory letter, make specific reference to your presentation expertise. If you can provide a few concrete examples based on one of the company's own presentations, all the better. ("As a professional communicator, I help add a measure of focus and impact to both internal and client-facing presentations. In the attached, for example, I've made half a dozen suggestions that I thought might enhance the presentation's overall effectiveness.")

Who Do I Contact?

Often, presentations published by a company will include the author's name, usually on the title page or at the end. There's nothing wrong with contacting these people directly. If you can't get a specific name, determine who to send your letter to based on the size of the company.

If it's a Small Fish or Lone Wolf, send it straight to the president or CEO. If it's a Big Dog, send it to the manager of the local office. Always call and get an individual name.

What Do I Charge?

For slides that aren't too text-heavy, fifteen minutes per slide is a fair rate; for denser ones, thirty minutes per slide. So, for example, if you've decided your corporate rate is $60 per hour, for a twenty-slide presentation your quote will be $300 for a text-light presentation (20 slides × 15 minutes per slide), $600 for a text-heavy one (20 slides × 30 minutes per slide).

MARKETING MATERIALS

Every company needs to promote itself. For the vast majority of organizations, this self-promotion occurs in the form of print materials consisting of words and images intended to communicate a particular story about a product or service to potential customers. The difference between hiring a professional writer to help tell the story and assigning someone internally to do it is the difference between focused copy that pops and aimless language that amounts to little more than a flat sales pitch. The decision makers within most companies don't always recognize this difference readily, but once an example of it crosses their desks, they tend to become permanent endorsers of the importance of investing in professional communicators like you.

The most common types of marketing materials are the brochures and flyers you receive in the mail every day. They come in myriad formats and styles, and they can look ultra-slick thanks to the fancy graphics and high-quality paper stock the marketing team has opted for, but that means a whole lot of nothing unless they also contain the right words. With the amount of such material most people receive every day, companies get exactly one shot to grab the attention of potential customers, and this they know all too well. That's why they're willing to invest whatever it takes to get it right.

45
MARKETING MATERIALS

With the amount of brochures, flyers, leaflets, and e-mail blasts most people get every day, companies know they have only one chance to seize customers' attention. That's why they're willing to invest in a professional wordsmith to get it right.

Get This Gig: Marketing Materials

Where Do I Start?

For a month, save every piece of direct mail you find in your mailbox. That will give you a healthy cross-section of brochures, flyers, and other types of marketing materials to practice on. Decide how well they tell the story they're trying to tell, how clearly they communicate, how consistent they sound. Then try to improve them.

In your introductory letter, call out marketing materials as one of your areas of expertise. Specializing in more specific areas, like speeches, can be a good way to distinguish yourself, but never cut yourself off from the broad panoply of marketing pieces all companies produce.

Who Do I Contact?

The companies sending you this stuff. If they can make unsolicited contact with you, there's no reason you can't do the same in return. If the mail pieces themselves contain names and contact information, target those people directly. If they don't, target according to the size of the company, as for presentations.

What Do I Charge?

Since marketing materials differ widely in tone and layout, use a general guideline of about one hour per every 250 words of writing or 500 words of editing.

Selling Yourself (THE RIGHT WAY)

Almost all writers share an aversion to self-marketing because they feel the superficial selling part undermines the authentic writing part. Here's the thing about that: There's no room for shyness in freelancing. Modesty, yes; shyness, no. Take a moment to think about it and you'll realize all businesspeople must market themselves just like writers do. A restaurateur needs to do more than just open his doors to generate traffic. An investment broker must go beyond merely getting a license if he hopes to succeed. A psychologist wanting to build a practice ought to take a few steps in addition to simply hanging a shingle. And a writer needs to do more than just write. "This job is about sales as much as it is about writing," says Toronto-based freelancer Ian Harvey. "One of the simple rules guiding my practice is this: Hustle, hustle, hustle."

So how does a writer generate buzz? There are several ways: letters, flyers, brochures, newsletters, blogs, samples, cold calls, and so on. Don't stop at your initial blitz. These days it's perfectly acceptable to let people know about things happening in your practice—new services you're offering, exciting projects you're working on, awards you've won—through social networking channels like LinkedIn, Facebook, and Twitter. People have become accustomed to receiving frequent updates from others. Use this to your advantage.

WHITE PAPERS

Just as companies need to promote their products and services, they also need to demonstrate that they know what they're talking about. So they often write and circulate white papers, reports, or guides that show off the company's smarts about a certain topic, issue, or problem. White papers take their name from the fact that they stand distinct from high-gloss marketing brochures. They're used ostensibly to educate readers and help people make decisions—though of course their ultimate purpose is to win customers. A white paper, for example, might focus on the benefits of a new product or technology. Or it might help elucidate a business process or concept for a lay audience. Or it might articulate a specialized solution to a pressing business need.

Regardless what they're attempting to market—manufacturing expertise, design brilliance, sales strategy, plain old intellectual capital—companies will often go to great expense to publish their white papers, since these documents must be accurate, authoritative, succinct, and forceful. They're meant to generate sales leads, establish thought leadership, make a business case, or educate customers. With such important goals, companies need a professional writer to get the job done properly.

46 WHITE PAPERS

The name may sound plain, but don't be fooled—white papers can be worth their weight in gold.

Get This Gig: White Papers

Where Do I Start?

Since they're created for the purpose of public consumption, white papers shouldn't be difficult to find. Google "white papers" and the name of your city or region and see what comes up. Or call your local chamber of commerce and ask for a listing of businesses in your area, then search based on that list. Go straight to the company Web site and start to dig; if that doesn't turn up anything of use, try doing a general search using "white papers" plus the company name.

It may be a good bit of strategy to include in your introductory letter an offer to write a white paper pro bono for prospective clients. Remember, you must adopt a long-term, big-picture mentality when thinking about your freelance career. Of greatest importance is to merely get a foot in the door. Once you've shown your stuff—even if it's for free the first time—the company knows it has a reliable resource for a long time to come.

Who Do I Contact?

Published white papers almost always include the author's name. That's who should receive the letter outlining your services and providing specific examples of how you can make an impressive piece even better.

What Do I Charge?

An hour per page is your goal. To get your foot in the door, maybe a half-hour per page.

SPEECHES

A great speech can be a career-maker; a dull speech, the opposite. A good writer takes the time to frame a speech within a specific structure, impose upon it a certain voice and tone, pace it according to a deliberate rhythm, and punctuate it with subtle moments of contrast or humor. Exceptional speeches are like superb pieces of music: They have great lyrics *and* a great melody.

It is to every writer's advantage that no one ever forgets the towering feeling of delivering a speech and knowing it made a lasting impression. In other words, write one speech that sings, and the person you wrote it for will tell everyone else on his team, or in his department, or around his executive conference table, that you've got the goods. And it isn't just the person who delivered the speech from whom you might get valuable recommendations. Just as often, those in the audience want to know who wrote those wonderful words, too.

"A professional communicator can transform the story you're trying to tell into something powerful and memorable."

—Gord Forfar, Senior Vice President, Personal & Commercial Product Operations, Bank of Montreal

Get This Gig: Speeches

Where Do I Start?

By positioning yourself specifically as a speechwriter. Don't send a letter saying you're a freelance writer who does it all, speeches included. People tend to perceive speechwriting as a discipline unto itself, so sell it that way. Enroll with Toastmasters International. Contact the National Speakers Bureau and ask what opportunities might be available. Tell middle-management or junior-associate friends you're willing to do some speech work for them pro bono so you can cite those credentials later.

Who Do I Contact?

Start with the president's executive assistant. The majority of speeches are given by the top names in any organization, and they aren't always satisfied with the copy their communications department comes up with. Furthermore, senior people like the feeling of having an individual resource they can depend on. When that resource is outside the company, the feeling of exclusivity can be even stronger. So aim for the top.

What Do I Charge?

An hour of your time for every three to five minutes of speaking is the appropriate range.

ANNUAL REPORTS

Public companies—that is, those owned by public shareholders like you and me—are obligated to publish a report every year that discloses where they stand money-wise and the direction they plan to take going forward. While these documents are data-heavy, they also include a considerable amount of writing, including, typically, the chairman and/or president's letter up front plus lots of captions, headings, legends, descriptions, and justifications. Few writers will tell you that annual reports are particularly exciting to write or edit, but consider that a company's annual report is the single most important document it will prepare during the year, and if the final result is something that makes everyone in the organization proud, everyone who worked on it will be thought of with that extra bit of glitter. Which, in your case, can lead to other assignments and positive word of mouth. And that's what it's all about.

48
ANNUAL REPORTS

A company's annual report may not be the most exciting thing it publishes all year, but it's certainly the most important.

Get This Gig: Annual Reports

Where Do I Start?

Every public company is legally bound to make its annual report available to the public. Many, in fact, are now published online. So take that list of local businesses you received from your local chamber of commerce and do a hard-target search of annual reports on their Web sites. If they aren't posted, call the company directly and ask to be sent a copy. Then, in your introductory letter, include annual reports among your specialty areas.

Who Do I Contact?

The annual report, though invariably a team effort, is most often owned by the marketing department. Send your letter to the marketing manager, marketing director, or vice president of marketing.

What Do I Charge?

Since the page-by-page content of annual reports is highly variable—one page might be almost all text, another might be almost all graphs—use an hourly rate. It's notoriously difficult to predict how many hours of your time annual reports are going to take, though more than expected is a safe bet.

OTHER REPORTS

The annual report aside, companies have a constant need to generate several other types of reports for the purpose of informing various audiences on the status of various projects. One of my clients, an information technology systems consulting firm, performs a monthly analysis for each of its clients on each desktop computer in the office as well as the overall computer network. They do a rigorous audit of functionality, speed, and performance, producing an internal report made up largely of number grids. Then they pay me to take all that data and turn it into language understandable to what I call the MIL: the Most Important Layperson in the office. Usually the MIL is a senior executive who is a far cry from tech-savvy but who has the decision-making power to just as easily green-light tech improvements as stop them dead in their tracks. This is just one example of the kind of report you might help companies produce. They spit out a lot of them—and someone like you can take the spit and use it to polish the report to a high shine.

49
OTHER REPORTS

With general reports, write for the MIL: the Most Important Layperson in the office. The MIL is not necessarily the highest-ranking person in the client office or the one with the most knowledge or expertise; it's the person who wields the most influence when it comes to your project.

Get This Gig: Other Reports

Where Do I Start?

Choose half a dozen local companies and go to their Web sites. Go to the tabs that say Services or What We Do or the closest such description you can find. There these organizations will talk about all the great services they offer, and you will find clues to the kinds of communications needs they have. Is it a management consulting firm? Then dollars to donuts they do umpteen presentations every month. A retail conglomerate? Odds are they produce marketing materials on a pretty much constant basis. Do this exercise with as many companies as you can, then tailor your initial contact letter accordingly.

Who Do I Contact?

Since the irregular reports companies produce don't fall into any specific category, make your contact strategy general as well. Contact the manager of human resources—send a great letter that outlines your skills and services, and cite examples of half a dozen different types of corporate writing you'd be happy to handle. With any luck, one of them will stick.

What Do I Charge?

It depends on the project, but an hourly rate is usually a good basis for your first go-round with a new company.

Dress the Part
(OF A PROFESSIONAL)

Writers have traditionally worn the "creative person's" outfit—the stereotypical turtleneck and suede jacket with elbow patches, or some other variation—perhaps in a deliberate attempt to separate themselves from the corporate, money-grubbing drones they disdain. Dispense with this idea, starting today. When you meet with a client or prospect, you aren't there to announce yourself as a counterculture icon, you're there to announce yourself as a professional with a valuable service to offer. You're in business, they're in business. Sometimes you're in business together. Sell the value of your services through both the quality of your work and the way you present yourself as a professional. If you get invited to a meeting for potential corporate work, err on the side of overdressing, unless you know for certain that the corporate environment you're entering is casual. Arriving in a suit when others are in shirts looks fine; arriving in a shirt when others are in suits does not.

 CONFERENCE SCRIPTS

Everyone loves a conference. It's a break from the normal office routine, it offers a chance to mingle with colleagues, and it provides the opportunity to stay at a fancy hotel for a night or two.

That's the perspective of those *attending* the conference. But to those *organizing* the conference, its significance is much weightier. This group must concern itself with communicating certain messages; ensuring smooth, logical transitions between sessions; and the hope that people will come away from the conference feeling united as a team and inspired to perform. After all, once the conference is done, it's going to be evaluated formally or informally, and the opinions of those who attended are going to wend their way to the executive or senior team who sponsored the conference. If it's a winner, all is golden; if not, the pall is cast. Bottom line: The organizing committee knows it had better do a good job.

And hopefully they know this: The success of any conference comes down to (a) how effectively it's structured overall, and (b) how well its individual elements are delivered. As a professional communicator, you have plenty to offer in this regard.

First, there's stepping back and figuring out what the conference is truly about. Most conference teams will dive in and start developing sessions, team-building exercises, and breakout discussions without a cohesive understanding of what they're actually trying to accomplish, like people trying to combine pieces from different jigsaw puzzles into a common one. Since your expertise is rooted in the ability to pull a single thread out of a bunch of disparate material, the best first step you can offer any conference organizers is to conduct a focused session whose sole reason is to answer the question, "What is the purpose of this conference?" You might be surprised how difficult it can be for them to agree on an answer. Once they do, you can help them plan an overall mix that accomplishes its goals.

That overall mix will be made up of numerous individual sessions to take place over the course of the conference, whether three hours or three days. Most people are not good presenters. Even fewer are good session leaders or facilitators. You can help further by working with them to storyboard presentations, brainstorm interactive activities, structure breakout sessions, and so on.

On a more granular level, you can help write the actual words people are going to say. A variety of people end up taking the podium at a conference, and the range of speaking skill is inevitably broad. Some people prefer being scripted down to the last word; others prefer having a general course laid out for them with the key points they need to hit along the way. Here's a rule of thumb: The more senior or experienced the person, the less scripted they'll want to be; the more junior or inexperienced, the more they'll appreciate your writing help. The person chairing the annual company sales conference, for instance, will probably be the vice president of sales or regional sales manager or some other comparable person who's done so before. That person will probably be happy to use your help planning the overall conference theme, the connections between sessions, and the creative breakouts. But there will also probably be, say, a junior sales associate new to the company who's been asked to do a presentation on his customers' responses to the product the company recently launched. That's a command performance, and no doubt a nerve-wracking one. The junior sales associate might have a decent idea of the messages he wants to get across but only a vague idea of how to do so. He'll be thrilled to have someone like you in his corner.

50
CONFERENCE SCRIPTS

A successful conference is just a topical story with multiple plot lines interwoven around a clear theme.

Get This Gig: Conference Scripts

Where Do I Start?

Conference scripting will be seen as a specialty, so create some marketing collateral that specifically calls out this service. It can be a letter, a simple flyer, or anything you feel communicates the message effectively.

Who Do I Contact?

There are two different parties you want to get in touch with. First, the human resources departments of all the companies on your list. All departments have conferences, retreats, and off-site meetings, so targeting any one of them amounts to a crapshoot, whereas Human Resources is the only department that touches every other department.

Second, make contact with event firms. These are companies in business for the express purpose of running events for other companies. They're typically full-service operations, meaning when they get hired to run a conference, they take on all the responsibilities of that conference, including concepts, scripts, and activities. Tell them how much you'd love to work with them and just how good a fit, given your skill set, it would be.

What Do I Charge?

Since conference writing involves a number of different facets, determine your fee via an accumulation of hours. To provide the most accurate quote possible, ask as many questions as you can and be perfectly clear on the scope of the assignment and what will be expected of you.

Someone Who Works for A BIG IMPORTANT COMPANY AND WHO HAS THE ABILITY TO HIRE FREELANCERS ANSWERS TEN IMPORTANT QUESTIONS

Nicole Bleiwas, Director of Customer, Commercial, and Consumer Leadership, Coca-Cola Ltd.

Q *When you're seeking a writer's help, what are the three most important characteristics you look for?*

Writing style, past experience, and cost.

Q *When you use freelance writers, how do you typically find them?*

Almost always through recommendations from others.

Q *Do you know at the outset of a project whether you'll need a writer, or is it usually a spontaneous call?*

I usually have a general idea that one may be required. The specific point during the project at which I engage a writer tends to be spontaneous.

Q *What's more important, a writer's rates or her credentials/experience?*

Credentials. There needs to be a value equation whereby rates and quality of work match up.

Q *Under what circumstances do you usually seek freelance or contract help?*

Usually for documents that are intended for broad distribution. If they're going to be seen by lots of eyes, they need to be done well.

Q *When enlisting freelancers, do you need to go through a lot of approval hoops?*

Our company has a policy for hiring vendors, and this applies to freelance writers just as it does other suppliers, like promotional agencies. Any outside individual must be willing to sign a nondisclosure agreement before we begin work with her.

Q *If a freelancer/contractor does solid work for you on one project, is there a good chance you'll go back to her for another one down the road?*

Yes. Definitely.

Q *What are the main advantages of using a professional writer/communications expert versus someone in-house?*

When using someone in-house, you run the risk of the communication being internally focused and therefore only understood by those within the company. So the intended audience plays a role in whether we go in-house or external.

Q *When checking a freelancer's credentials, where's the first place you go (e.g., her Web site, paper samples, calling references)?*

I like to look at samples of the person's work.

Q *What's the number one thing a freelancer can do to get in, and stay in, your good books?*

Listen to objectives and follow the brief.

CORPORATE VIDEOS

When launching a new strategy, implementing a new system, announcing a new initiative, or rolling out a new program, companies of a certain size face a sticky problem: how to communicate the change, and its importance, to all of their employees. Sometimes this is done through the distribution of gargantuan binders that no one reads but everyone displays on their cubicle shelves. Sometimes it's done via extensive orientation sessions. Other times it's conveyed with a long memo from the CEO outlining how strongly she feels about the new initiative.

Sometimes, however, the top brass decide to create a video to communicate the change, and sometimes—that is, when the right writer is used—that video marries stylishness with intelligence, resulting in a replicable tool that engages people in a way they find entertaining and informative. Such videos aren't usually long—five to ten minutes is pretty typical—but they are carefully assembled, usually with the help of the company's graphics and information technology personnel. They sometimes include messages of support from the project sponsors or testimonials from employees, interspersed with critical information about the new program and what it means for the company and its people.

Corporate videos are great fun to work on because (a) they typically entail a large investment from the top, so those assigned to both the creative and production teams treat the work seriously and want to do a great job, (b) it's one of those writing projects that involves high-energy, high-spirited collaboration, (c) seeing the end product often produces a great sense of accomplishment and gratification, and (d) writing a script is always fun, no matter what you're writing it for.

51 CORPORATE VIDEOS

A corporate video helps the company sell itself to its customers and its employees.

Get This Gig: Corporate Videos

Where Do I Start?

Though corporate videos are a great potential addition to your list of credits, they aren't produced frequently enough to warrant a specifically tailored letter. So take the standard letter you use to introduce yourself to corporate prospects and make sure it includes mention of corporate videos.

Who Do I Contact?

Any corporate videos will be joint efforts between Marketing and Information Technology, so send your communiqué to the heads of both departments.

What Do I Charge?

It depends on your level of involvement. You might be asked to write an introduction and nothing else. Or you might be asked to conduct interviews with people across the organization and then edit the transcripts of those interviews into catchy three-minute vignettes. Or somewhere in between. As always, be clear up front on what you're being asked to deliver and then deliver a quote that assumes 20 percent more hours than you—or they—would likely expect.

INTERNAL MEMOS

A company isn't likely to enlist your services strictly to write an internal memo, but once you're in the door and have proven that any document you touch becomes better, don't be surprised if the people on the teams you work with start to come to you for other stuff. A memo from a junior associate to her supervisor, for example, may seem of minor significance to you, but to her it might mean the difference between getting a big project approved or rejected—and getting it approved might mean a move to the next level, and a move to the next level might mean a substantial raise or a critical foothold toward eventual partnership. I derive tremendous pleasure when clients approach me for help with increasingly small assignments, not because it feeds my ego but because it tells me that they've come to appreciate the true mountain-moving power of professional communications. Getting in can be a challenge, sure, but I don't know of any client who, after discovering the impact a trained communicator can make, has ever looked back.

52 INTERNAL MEMOS	"No matter how small or insignificant it might seem, every time you communicate, it matters." —Edward Hughes, President and CEO, Aculon Inc.

Get This Gig: Internal Memos

Where Do I Start?

Whenever you're working for a client in their offices for any stretch of time, you'll inevitably be copied on lots of memos. Keep the e-mails, memos, and other notices you get, and try to gather other ones, too, like those sitting on top of the recycle bin or unclaimed for an entire day at the side of the photocopier. Take them home and review them in detail to see if any common flaws are detectable. Eventually you can have a casual chat with the department manager about the fact that interdepartmental communications seem slightly marred, and you have a few suggestions for ironing them out.

Who Do I Contact?

No one at first. This is, as I said, an inside job, and you need to be the insider. Don't send a letter to a company telling them you want to write their internal memos. Wait until you've gained access to the inner sanctum, then do your homework and figure out who has both the right level of authority and the right amount of trust in your opinion.

What Do I Charge?

Little, if anything. This is the kind of work you do to cement your reputation and enhance your perceived value. If you're asked to, say, create new interdepartmental communications templates, that's a project, and you should charge accordingly. But if the executive responsible for your check asks you occasionally to review the memo she wants to send out, don't go send an invoice.

B2B PUBLICATIONS

You've probably heard the term B2B. It stands for Business to Business (as opposed to B2C, which stands for Business to Consumer). Many companies produce specific marketing materials targeted not at the general public but at other companies they hope to turn into customers. A company that manufactures computer parts, for instance, may market itself to the consumer at large, but it's more likely to invest dollars in marketing to other businesses, who are most likely to have use for its products and would place bigger orders on a more regular basis.

One of my clients is a designer and producer of office interiors. Though its products are displayed in retail showrooms across the country, its marketing efforts are solely B2B—that is, they're targeted strictly at other businesses from whom they stand to win big contracts, as opposed to a one-man show like me, someone who might buy a desk or chair only once every few years. They know where their bread is buttered, and they strategize accordingly. Because companies invest substantially in B2B programs and the materials that support them, professional writers are a critical resource for them. The competition for customers rages daily and is more concentrated today than ever before. Organizations recognize that if they aren't getting their message out properly, they might as well not be getting it out at all.

53 B2B PUBLICATIONS	B2B (Business to Business) materials are those that companies send to other companies to try to turn them into customers. All organizations know that the competition is fierce, so the writing has to be powerful.

Get This Gig: B2B Publications

Where Do I Start?

If you have friends, associates, or former colleagues employed at companies who conduct B2B marketing, ask if they can sneak you a sample or two so you can get familiar with the look and sound of typical B2B materials. Short of that, it's difficult to perform targeted B2B research because most companies' B2B efforts are internal and proprietary. The most sensible way to advertise your B2B offering is to simply include it among the other services noted in your introductory letter.

Who Do I Contact?

Send your letter to marketing managers at Big Dogs, Small Fish, and Lone Wolves, all of whom work in the B2B space.

What Do I Charge?

B2B writing, like most other corporate writing assignments, will involve specific amounts of copy for specific marketing pieces. Base your estimate on the general number of words you expect to write, and use a guideline of an hour for every 250 words of fresh writing or 500 words of editing.

MANUALS AND TECHNICAL WRITING

Those in engineering departments, on product development teams, and, especially, in technology roles adore people who can describe the things they design and manufacture in terms decipherable to the layperson. One of my clients devises surveillance systems using artificial intelligence software; I write scripts for the Flash videos they post on their Web site that let people see how cool and effective their products are. The people at this company are brilliant, but they all think and communicate in complex terms intimidating to, say, an airport manager who just wants to know whether their system is going to help him catch suspicious characters. That's where writers come in. The faster technology and manufacturing race forward, the greater the need for people who can say things clearly. Picture yourself tearing open the box to a new purchase—a computer, a bike, an electronic toy—and, as the instruction booklet flies out and you snatch it, think of the difference in your reactions toward instructions filled with convoluted steps and impossible-to-decipher diagrams vs. simple, unambiguous directions laid out in plain language and accompanied by corresponding drawings. The difference in those two reactions is the difference between a professional writer and anybody else.

54 MANUALS AND TECHNICAL WRITING

Being able to write complicated things in a simple way is like being the only person in a room who can translate a foreign language.

Get This Gig: Manuals and Technical Writing

Where Do I Start?

Whenever you receive a new product, keep the diagram or instructions that accompany it. Fortunately, such documents almost always contain errors, or at the very least language that barely warrants being called language. Next, prepare a specific letter offering your technical writing services in a casual, friendly way. Make note of the diagram or instructions you received and gently point out a spot or two in which things might have been communicated a little more clearly.

Who Do I Contact?

Send your letter to the company's marketing manager or director, since the piece was most likely produced by her department.

What Do I Charge?

It's been my experience that technical writing takes considerably longer than people assume it will, in part because those who need to approve the copy are often big-time sticklers about how the details are conveyed. Be aware of this when quoting so you don't shortchange yourself.

PACKAGE COPY

Gum, potato chips, batteries, lightbulbs, contact lenses, radish seeds—anything sold for consumer purchase is in some way packaged, and those packages almost always contain some writing. Don't believe me? Next time you're pushing your shopping cart through the grocery store (and trying to resist popping a wheelie), take a moment to inspect every item you toss in. Words are everywhere. Sure, sometimes those words are no more complicated than "Excellent Source of Vitamin C," but often they're much more than that. Think of the typical kids' cereal box. Yes, the side tells you how much of your child's daily riboflavin quotient he's getting, but the back is usually filled with fun, varied copy, from mazes to trivia to contests.

The writing that ends up on packages is normally the result of a highly sensitive dance between a company's legal and marketing departments, the former concerned with obligatory copy like ingredients, best before date, manufacturer's address, and so on, the latter concerned with copy that will actually, you know, help sell the product. The great thing about your freelance role is that you don't need to take up arms for one side or the other. Instead you get to be the golden child who makes them both happy.

55 PACKAGE COPY	Just about anything sold has a package—and just about any package has words.

Get This Gig: Package Copy

Where Do I Start?

Begin with a fun exercise. Go through your shelves and pull out every single item that has words on it. For instance, at the moment there is a bag of Lay's potato chips on my desk. I'm about to devour, oh, the entire bag, I imagine, but in the meantime I'm reading the back: "It starts with quality, homegrown potatoes, just as it always has ..." This goes on for four paragraphs, or about 75 words. I can tell those 75 words weren't easy to compose, and I bet they went through several levels of approval before making it onto that bag. They're precisely the kind of words companies love assigning to freelancers, since doing so releases the marketing people who shouldn't have been writing copy in the first place, plus they get the comfort of knowing it's being done by a professional.

Next, prepare a list of the companies who manufacture all those items you've pulled out of the cupboard. These are packaged goods (also called consumer goods) companies. Their name has to be included on every product they manufacture, so if you can't find it right away, keep looking. Craft a targeted letter whose body talks about your specialization writing package copy. Then visit each of the company's Web sites so you can tweak each letter by making specific reference to their products, history, culture, or recent successes.

Who Do I Contact?

Call each company's head office and get the name of its marketing manager, then send off the letters to as many companies on your initial list as you can. Cast enough lines and you're bound to get some bites.

What Do I Charge?

Determine a small range for your hourly rate, and quote based on the size of the company. Lay's is a Big Dog, so I would charge them the rate at the top end of my range. For Small Fish and Lone Wolves I would charge closer to the bottom end.

Ten Questions WITH PAUL LIMA

Paul Lima, author of *The Six-Figure Freelancer,* is one of the fellow freelancers I most admire because of his unwaveringly disciplined approach to the writing profession and his ongoing self-challenge to broaden his expertise and expand his services. Here are Paul's thoughts on a few matters:

Q *Name three factors that have contributed to your freelance success.*

One: desire. I wanted to run a freelance writing business. Two: dedication. When the work is there, I dedicate time to complete it. When the work isn't there, I dedicate time to find it. Three: discipline. The first couple of years were tough. I could have quit. But I remained focused on the task of making it as a freelancer.

Q *If you could go back and visit yourself when you were first starting out in the business, what advice would you give?*

"Sales" is not a dirty word. Realize you are running a business and that selling and marketing is an integral part of any business. If you are not selling yourself, your abilities, and your services, nobody is.

Q *What are the most common mistakes you see freelancers making when approaching corporate markets?*

They don't develop a business vision—who they are, what they sell, and who they should sell to. They don't spend any time thinking about the services they can offer or the sectors they should target. Focus your marketing: Sell services you can deliver to sectors you're familiar with. If an offer to do something you've never done for a sector you've never written for comes your way, look at it and take it if you think you can do it. But don't try to sell writing services you aren't familiar with to sectors you have no knowledge of.

Q *Why is writing and communications expertise so important to companies today?*

Every company needs to communicate with customers, vendors, suppliers, and staff. More and more of that communication is electronic writing—e-mail, Web sites, intranets, blogs, social networking. However, even if the communication is on paper or by voice, the words must speak to the reader and achieve the business objectives of the company or organization. It takes a skilled writer to pull that off.

Q *What are you continually trying to improve in your own practice?*

I create a business plan every year, and I don't just pick up last year's plan and try to do more of the same. I try to add new components that are of interest to me and that I believe will generate new revenue. In other words, I don't want to ever become complacent.

Q *What are your biggest flaws as a freelancer? What do you struggle with the most?*

My grade five teacher will tell you: I'm a poor speller and I don't know many of the rules of grammar. Seriously. However, I know how to structure a document and clearly communicate my client's purpose. I hire proofreaders to help compensate for my weaknesses.

Q *In what ways have you reconciled the aversion to self-marketing that afflicts so many creative people?*

Having a family, a car, a mortgage, and a dog that eats more than the family helps me reconcile my aversion to self-marketing. In other words, I know how much I have to earn per year, and I know how much I have to earn per week to hit my annual revenue goal. I also know that money does not fall like manna from heaven.

Q *What attributes would you say keep your corporate clients coming back?*

When I am writing, I deliver the right words—on time and on budget. I also check my ego at the door. If the client wants a revision, I discuss the rationale for it, make a few comments, and let the client decide which way we go based on a sound understanding of the target audience and objective of the document we are working on. I also do some business writing training. I demonstrate practical techniques and tools that help my clients become more effective and efficient writers. My objective is a satisfied client who will hire me again and refer me to other prospects.

Q *Do you have what you would call a daily routine?*

I wake up and go to work! What I have to do each day is in my calendar. I turn on my computer and do not go to e-mail or the Web. I go to my calendar first. I've set it up to tell me what to do based on my business priorities. It all goes back to discipline. Discipline and time management start with knowing what you want to do, and why. I've written eight books in the last five years and am working on two more—all while running a full-time freelance writing and training business.

Q *What are the most common obstacles you face when trying to market your services to companies? What have you done to overcome these obstacles?*

Like many writers, I don't like cold calls. So I send letters or e-mails first. Then when I call the prospects, I am not making cold calls—I'm following up!

NEWSLETTERS

The first corporate gig I ever had was writing copy for an internal newsletter at Procter & Gamble. My mom was a sales manager there, and she'd somehow finagled me a summer job assisting one of the people who worked for her, a wonderfully elegant French woman who I seem to remember wore terrific necklaces. She wanted to communicate her

division's projects, priorities, and achievements to the rest of the staff on an ongoing basis.

This occurs frequently within corporations of a certain size: Not only does the company as a whole try to market itself to consumers, but departments within the company try to market themselves to other departments so that (a) everyone can see how valuable their work is, thereby creating job security for everyone on the team, (b) their individual accomplishments get highlighted and land on the radar screens of those who ultimately make decisions about things like promotions, and (c) they stay "top of mind" even when their services aren't in immediate need. Newsletters are the best way to accomplish quick, regular communication both external and internal, and these days they're cropping up everywhere. Even small businesses are distributing newsletters to let you know what they're up to and what they think about certain matters—no doubt you receive several—either in paper or electronic form.

The positive news for writers is that newsletters are typically more involved than they seem. That snippet about the new product the company is unveiling next month may be allotted only 250 words, but it ain't an easy 250 words. Consider that various departments reading the newsletter will likely have a different level of familiarity with the product and that, in those few words, the big cheeses are going to want to see the product's benefits well articulated and its position in the marketplace made clear—all while the whole enchilada is subtly placed within the context of the company's strategic vision so the staff gets excited about the product launch.

In other words, it takes a professional's hand. One thing that continues to delight and inspire me is how much people really do notice the difference between first-rate writing and other writing once both pass before them. This plays out powerfully in companies, because people trying to gain a leg up in the rat race realize that every small advantage has enormous implications.

Newsletters are also good examples of seemingly small writing projects that can generate a surprisingly large ripple effect. Unlike the binders handed out at most conferences that get placed spine out on cubicle shelves but never get read, people actually read newsletters, since they are by nature easy to digest and quick to finish. Or, if it helps to think about it another way, understand that, when people read a newsletter for which you've written copy, they're reading your writing. And if there's one principle that holds for novels, haiku, or corporate newsletters, it's this: The greater number of people who read your writing, the more likely you are to garner a broader swath of interest. Treat everything you write with equal importance, because you never know who's going to read it. One of my proudest moments in the corporate arena was a colleague saying, "I.J., these are the best meeting minutes I've ever read." Yep—I'd worked my butt off to make them sound right.

Newsletters are great examples of seemingly small projects that can generate large ripple effects.

Get This Gig: Newsletters

Where Do I Start?

You probably delete requests asking you to sign up for company newsletters so summarily that you don't realize how many of them there actually are. From now on, sign up for all of them. When they arrive, read them closely and think about what you could do improve them. Then tailor your introductory letter to include prominent mention of newsletter writing, researching, and editing. As you accumulate newsletter credits, you can cite them in the letter.

Who Do I Contact?

For each newsletter you receive, call the company and ask who coordinates it. Send that person your standard introductory letter. If you don't hear anything back, follow up a few weeks later by phone.

What Do I Charge?

As for most marketing materials, a general guideline of an hour for every 250 words of writing or 500 words of editing should serve you well.

RELEASES

When a company wants to put the word out about something but doesn't want to break the bank on advertising, they issue a press release (also called a media release, news release, event release, product press release, and, increasingly today, social media release—the terms are largely interchangeable). This is sometimes referred to as sending it "over the wire," an allusion to wire services like Reuters whose job it is to trawl for stories and broadcast the ones considered most noteworthy to the public through a variety of channels. A company might send its press release to a journalist at a specific newspaper. It might e-mail the release to an entire customer database. It might fax the release to a select group of B2B clients. It might do all three, and then some.

It depends ultimately what, on the company's behalf, the release is trying to achieve. If you think about a release as someone standing up in the middle of a party and shouting, "I have an announcement, everyone!" it will be easier to write one. If that person is announcing that they've invented a new pill even better than Viagra, the announcement is going to take a certain tone and be of interest to a certain audience. If they're announcing that Brangelina have confirmed they're coming to the town's film festival next month, the announcement will have a different pitch and be targeted toward a different segment of the population.

Releases have a fairly rigid structure, whether you're writing about the opening of a swanky new local restaurant or the location of the next Olympic Games. They provide, in an extremely straightforward fashion, enough basic information that those receiving it have enough to follow up on if they're so inclined. The basic structure of a release contains the following elements: headline (grab their attention), dateline (the date of the release and the city from which it originated), introduction (the five Ws), body (other details to whet readers' whistles), boilerplate (usually the "About" paragraph that gives info about the issuing organization or individual), close (usually the -30- symbol or ###), and contact info (to let people know who they can contact for more information, since that, after all, is what you're hoping the release will accomplish in the first place). Often a reinforcing quote is included as well.

Since releases are designed to provide information rather than entertain, they're excellent outlets for demonstrating your mastery of language and showing off your ability to transmit information in a logical, structured, concise way. Creative flair isn't usually welcome in releases—though, again, it depends on what's being announced. If you're writing about something edgy, funny, hip, or somehow outside the norm, it may be appropriate to stretch the rules of the form slightly, but always make the argument and get permission first. Otherwise, stick to convention.

57 RELEASES	Releases are a simple, straightforward way for companies to let the public know about noteworthy developments. But they still have to be written well.

Get This Gig: Releases

Where Do I Start?

Many organizations have a fairly frequent need for release writing, so be sure to mention this skill prominently in at least one version of your introductory letter.

Who Do I Contact?

Releases are initiated and approved by the marketing department, so the person to aim for is the marketing manager or director.

What Do I Charge?

Release writing is fundamentally less complex than most other corporate materials, but the research required for their content is sometimes demanding, so consider it a wash and stick with a guideline of one hour per 250 words of writing or 500 words of editing.

 BIOS

Once they reach a certain level within a company, people need to have their bios at the ready. Either the company needs to post the bio on its Web site under "The Team," "Leadership," or "The People That Make Us Tick," or the bios are necessary for inclusion in client proposals. Or perhaps they need to be forwarded to a selection committee if the individual is being considered for an award. These are just a few examples; there are more. In most companies, anyone at an executive level requires a bio, but in many organizations these days such traditional thinking is tossed out the window and bios are done for individuals at multiple levels so the company can show how valued and expert all of its staff are. When I worked at McKinsey & Company, a mammoth management consulting firm charging equally mammoth fees, project teams were composed of an individual from every level, from senior partner down to business analyst—and you'd better believe the prospective client wanted to know about every single one of those people before it shelled out for the firm's services. The bios were each only a few paragraphs long, but each had to be compelling in its own right. In other words, they needed a writer's touch.

Like so many forms of writing, bios can be more challenging than they may at first blush appear. First, it's important to know what kind of personality the company wishes to convey so you're aware which would be preferred between "Frank earned his Ph.D. in Economics from Harvard" and "Frank eats all the cookies in the office, but he's ridiculously smart, so we keep him around." Second, you'll often be asked to compose multiple bios requiring consistent tone and structure but each sounding unique and portraying the individual in a special way. Finally, people's accomplishments and credentials change over time, so you may be asked to provide bios that sound distinct but also work as templates so new information can be plugged in later. For an architectural client of mine I was asked to write bios for everyone in the company, to make them sound "professional but lighthearted and fun," and to make sure all the relevant information was captured but not to make them too long so they could fit neatly on the Web site.

That's the kind of convoluted direction you should embrace, because once you prove you can deliver on it, you'll be perceived as someone who can write whatever the company needs whenever they need it—just the perception you want to achieve.

58 BIOS	"Bios are one of the first things customers read. You can't afford not to get them right." —Ted Matthews, Brand Coach

Get This Gig: Bios

Where Do I Start?

Do a random surf for company Web sites in your area, and home in on the bios they include. Read them for grammar, overall effectiveness, tonal and stylistic consistency with the rest of the Web site, and meaningfulness. Frequently this is where companies get tripped up. Do the bios seem to just float on their own with no connection to the rest of the site? Make notes for the bios on as many company sites as possible, then, when preparing your introductory letter, make mention of the fact that part of your expertise is optimizing the impact of every aspect of a company's Web site, including bios.

Who Do I Contact?

Call each company and request contact information for its Webmaster or, failing that, its head of IT. Both types of people, since they're at the other end of the creative spectrum, welcome the help of writers, just as writers welcome the help of technical support.

What Do I Charge?

The trick with bios is to make them different while also making sure they include all necessary information. This sometimes translates to more hours than expected. A typical bio, for example, might be only 50 words long, but it probably merits an hour for the actual writing and another half hour to call or e-mail the bio subject and glean usable information.

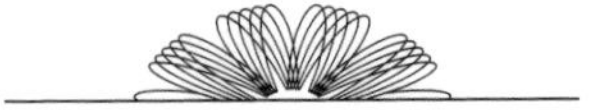

A Little Free Time GOES A LONG WAY

Here's a valuable tip: For your first assignment with a new client, identify something on your invoice as gratis. For instance, on all my initial invoices with a first-time client, if there are any extra rounds of editing beyond the first two (which are part of my standard agreement), I waive the fee for those extra rounds. Or I offer them a first-project 15 percent discount. It helps me be remembered as someone who looks out for his clients.

COMPANY HISTORIES/PROFILES

Organizations are constantly seeking ways to appear more genuine to their customers. One of the most common ways is to present a company history, typically showing the company's humble roots, its period of growth and expansion, and the fact that it continues to uphold the core values on which it was founded despite having become bigger than its creators ever dreamed. Or something to that effect. The point is that the company history/profile, in contrast to more straight-ahead business documents, is meant to work on a warmer, more intimate level. Its purpose is to show customers that the organization is run by real people and always has been, people who have worked hard to make the organization the best it can be and its products or services truly useful to other real people. The company history/profile, in other words, is an example of a kind of corporate writing that can have as much emotional impact as a finely crafted short story. It has the same elements, after all: characters striving to achieve a goal, a narrative arc, pivotal plot points, and a resolution.

Company histories/profiles also give you the chance to exhibit your innate ability to find, within reams of ordinary information, the more interesting story, the nuggets that will fascinate, the anecdotal gems that will amuse and inspire. When company histories/profiles are written by those inside the company walls, they often come out brutally dry, dominated by dates and figures (the company was founded in 1966, it reached a million dollars in sales by 1981, it opened its fiftieth store in 2002) instead of the truly interesting material, featuring—wait for it—the *people* who have made the company what it is today. Facts and figures are essential, but they work best when placed in the context of real people striving to do something great. Here's an excerpt from the timeline posted on the Ben & Jerry's corporate Web site:

> 1963
>
> Ben Cohen and Jerry Greenfield meet in seventh grade gym class in Merrick, New York (Long Island).
>
> 1977
>
> Ben and Jerry move to Vermont and complete a $5 correspondence course in ice cream-making from Penn State (they get a perfect score because the test is open book).

This is, in my view, an example of writing at its best, provided you look past the grammar. (That parenthetical sentence should be on its own, like this one.) In impressively few words, the writer has painted a portrait of two likeable, ambitious kids who don't take themselves too seriously but do take their business idea very seriously. Consider how out of place a dull, fact-and-figure-dominated timeline would seem on the Web site of such a fun company. No matter what you're asked to write, always get clarity and confirmation first on the voice in which it should be written. Then do your stuff.

59 COMPANY HISTORIES/ PROFILES	A company history/profile shows potential customers where the company has been, and, more importantly, where it's headed.

Get This Gig: Company Histories/Profiles

Where Do I Start?

You know all that surfing you did to find and examine company bios? Go back to the bookmarked company pages and see if they have a corporate history/profile posted. If not, prepare a unique letter that talks only about your specialty in writing company histories/profiles. Mention that most companies these days have their history summarized, if not detailed, on their Web sites, and that you have, for many of your clients, helped transform such summaries from simple timelines into vivid, engaging stories.

Who Do I Contact?

The company Webmaster or head of IT. Both are under terrific pressure these days to design Web sites that customers find appealing and informative. A professional writer offering them such a great idea might tickle them silly.

What Do I Charge?

It depends largely on how much research is involved. Usually it will land at one of three levels. Level 1: The company has a lot of already-organized content for you to go through and then create the story. Level 2: The company has reams of unorganized content from different sources, in different formats, written at different times, for you to go through and then create the story. Level 3: The company has little content and is dependent on you to talk to whomever you need to and find out whatever you can in order to create the story. Obviously, Level 1 will entail the simplest effort on your part, and Level 3 the greatest effort. Quote accordingly, always adding 20 percent more hours than your baseline estimate.

CASE STUDIES/PROJECT PROFILES

Talking the talk is easy. Any company can claim it's great at what it does. The real question is how to convince customers the company puts its money where its mouth is.

One way to accomplish this is by creating mini-stories around recent successes the company has had. These are often captured as attractive one-page presentation-style pieces, or, sometimes, as simple Word documents. Typically they follow a structure that describes the client, the problem, the company's approach to the problem, the solution it provided, and the positive results obtained from that solution. Case studies/project profiles show the company's value proposition in action. In other words, they show potential customers that the company walks the walk. The other great thing about them is that new ones come up all the time—and they aren't going to write themselves.

60 CASE STUDIES/ PROJECT PROFILES	Case studies/project profiles show that the company doesn't just talk the talk—it walks the walk, too.

Get This Gig: Case Studies/Project Profiles

Where Do I Start?

Case studies/project profiles are of greatest value to Small Fish and Lone Wolves. Big Dogs tend not to need them because of their already large customer base. In your letter or marketing kit targeted to these small- and medium-sized players, add a clear and concrete bit that includes (a) how much value can be derived from well-written case studies/project profiles, and (b) the fact that they just happen to be one of your specialty services.

Who Do I Contact?

Case studies/project profiles are marketing pieces, so send your stuff to the marketing manager.

What Do I Charge?

Again, this is a two-pronged exercise. There's the up-front work, involving meetings or correspondence with those from whom you need to gather information or with whom you need to collaborate on format and presentation (the in-house graphic designer, for example), and there's the actual writing. Show both parts in your estimate.

CUSTOMER STORIES/TESTIMONIES

Companies can spend a gazillion dollars on slick advertising, but they all know nothing beats a direct recommendation from one customer to another. That's why firms of every size are constantly trying to get customers to go on record and talk about how sublime their experience with the company or its products was. This isn't easy, however—consumers are happy to purchase things, but not many of them are willing to be mouthpieces for a company just to help it boost its bottom line.

With the right approach, however, those who act as buffers between company and customer can sometimes more easily convince the latter to offer a positive word or two about the former. And if it can be done for one company, it can be done for many.

61

CUSTOMER STORIES/ TESTIMONIES

"Customer stories are very powerful, but they must be written in an engaging way, like a good magazine article. Play up the drama, the challenge that was overcome, the mystery that was solved. Too many customer stories are wooden."

—Gordon Graham, freelancer

Get This Gig: Customer Stories/Testimonies

Where Do I Start?

Develop a process for obtaining customer stories/testimonies and a template for capturing them. It isn't enough just to mention in your introductory letter that you "write customer stories and testimonies." If the company can't convince its customers to talk, that's of no use. You need to sell yourself as someone who can both get the information (and the permission) and write the stories. There are plenty of ways to go about this, but regardless of the method you use, it must be seriously buttoned-down, since you only get one shot at it. As a starting point, take a look at *Stories That Sell* by Casey Hibbard, a book that talks all about drawing powerful stories out of satisfied customers and includes a specific chapter on securing consent.

Who Do I Contact?

Being able to tell the president that customer stories/testimonies are in hand and authorized would be a major feather in any marketer's cap. So aim directly for the marketing manager.

What Do I Charge?

Develop a specific pricing schedule and include it in the letter, flyer, or brochure you send to the marketing manager. Because customer stories/testimonies are tough to get, it's okay to attach a fair cost to them—$500, say, for getting an individual testimony and writing it up. This cost would increase if you are to place the text in presentation-ready format, too.

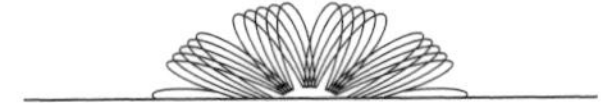

You and THE WORLD WIDE WEB

The debate over whether you need a Web site is long over. You need one. The first place people go to learn about any business today is the Internet, so don't think twice about the investment a Web site requires.

The good news: The investment can be quite small and still effective. The best writers' sites I know are the simplest, cleanest, and most straightforward. You're in the business of words, not graphics, so it's words, not graphics, that should be the strength of your site. Check out the Web sites of other writers and see which elements you find compelling and which you find forgettable. Use this investigation to decide how your site should look and what it should contain. Then, for a few hundred dollars, you can have a site that stands up to anyone else's and an ongoing online presence that helps convert curiosity into contracts.

 FAQS

There are two reasons most companies include a Frequently Asked Questions tab on their Web site: to let people know more about how the company operates, and to try to minimize the number of inquiries to Customer Service. If asked to do an FAQ exercise, be cognizant that people *inside* a company don't necessarily have an accurate handle on what people *outside* the company want to know. The best way to ascertain this is to not to talk to the people who run the business but to put yourself in the shoes of a potential or existing customer. Your goal is to help the company deliver what it needs—or, more frequently, wants.

FAQs can be short or long, serious or funny, static or dynamic. As with any corporate writing you do, the tone of your copy should match the personality of the organization. Before you write a word or perform a stitch of research, establish with your client what the FAQ is intended to achieve and what it should sound like, then off to the races you go. And don't underestimate the importance of an FAQ assignment. To your client, anything that makes the company more customer-friendly is nothing short of invaluable.

62 FAQS	Well-considered FAQs make the company seem more friendly to its customers—and you can't put a price on that.

Get This Gig: FAQs

Where Do I Start?

Search Web sites of companies engaged in more complex business offerings, like finance or technology. These are the companies that are going to naturally have the hardest time communicating clearly with their customers, and therefore will be the companies most sorely in need of a way to lay things out simply. Note the ones that don't have an FAQ or something analogous. Customize your introductory letter so it makes special mention of FAQs, then send it off to those companies.

Who Do I Contact?

The Webmaster or head of IT.

What Do I Charge?

FAQs, like press releases, aren't difficult in execution, but the process of obtaining the information you need from those who have it is not always smooth or well facilitated. Often you will need to gather bits and pieces from various internal sources and then synthesize it—seamlessly, of course. Before quoting, try to ask the kinds of questions that determine how extensive your grunt work will be prior to the actual writing: Does an FAQ for the company exist today in any form? How old is it? Who wrote it? What kinds of questions does the company's customer service team get asked most often?

BUCKSLIPS

Usually about the size of a dollar bill (hence the name), buckslips are small inserts added to larger mailing packages. Companies use them to call attention to a specific message or aspect within the context of something broader, like a special early bird offer within an overall promotion or an ad for a separate product that complements the main one being advertised (for example, a buckslip for a golf cart added to a golf store's monthly newsletter). Since they're usually printed on light paper, buckslips are a useful, cost-effective way to communicate late-breaking information or eleventh-hour changes, especially when the alternative is to alter and reprint an entire package.

63

BUCKSLIPS

Buckslips are usually short, containing at most a few hundred words of copy, so they need to be subtle and precise. In other words, they demand expertise like the kind you can offer.

Get This Gig: Buckslips

Where Do I Start?

Hold on to any and all buckslips you receive in the mail. Make notes about what you see as their most common flaws or shortcomings. Once you've completed this research, add a mention of buckslips to your introductory letter.

Who Do I Contact?

Buckslips are marketing materials, so go straight for the marketing jugular. In other words, send your letter to the marketing manager or director.

What Do I Charge?

Base your quote on the number of words the buckslip contains. The standard guideline—an hour for every 250 words of writing or every 500 words of editing—should be safe.

EVENT MATERIALS

From small customer appreciation events run by midsize firms to trade shows occupying entire floors of convention centers to elaborate galas sponsored by ginormous multinational conglomerates, just about every company takes part, in one capacity or another, in events of various kinds. These events can afford numerous opportunities for writers, because they need to be (a) advertised in advance with things like posters, flyers, invitations, and e-mail blasts, (b) highlighted during the event itself with things like notes, signs, banners, posters, demos, and presentations, and (c) followed up on with things like letters, thank-you cards, informal surveys, and materials promoting the following year's event.

Client requests for event-related writing might start out small, but be sure to knock every one of those small requests out of the park just as you would any big project, because events happen all the time, and what starts small may just get bigger, and bigger, and ... well, you get the idea.

64 EVENT MATERIALS	Event materials—from posters to flyers, invitations to presentations, thank-you cards to evaluation forms—offer no shortage of opportunities for writers.

Get This Gig: Event Materials

Where Do I Start?

Undertake a twin effort. First, do a Google search of "event companies"—companies that organize events on behalf of other organizations—plus your city. Then create a customized version of your introductory letter specifically targeting these companies and emphasizing your desire to work with event organizers.

Second, look for companies whose names show up on events in your area—golf tournaments, charity galas, that sort of thing. To those companies, send a version of your introductory letter that includes mention of event writing.

Who Do I Contact?

Go to the Web sites of the companies you find, or call their offices, and get the name of the person in charge of putting together event materials.

What Do I Charge?

If you're working on only one part of the overall event mix, the company you're working with may want to integrate your cost as part of its overall invoice. If you're writing event materials directly for the company organizing the event, charge according to your regular hourly rate.

DISPLAY/EXHIBIT MATERIALS

Go visit any nearby store and walk around. Take a mental inventory of every word you see displayed—on signs, stickers, banners, flyers, panels, cards, and so on. Most of the words you see in these displays come in the form of short phrases or pithy messages. Guess what? Someone had to write them. Words can move mountains, yes, but in the eyes of most companies what's more important is that they can move customers—into the store, and then toward certain products or displays. Often these words are part of displays or in-store promotions into which big bucks have been pumped from Head Office, so errors are certainly not acceptable, and neither is soft or aimless writing. Never measure the worth of an assignment by the number of words it involves. Every brilliant MBA graduate who has tried his hand at writing the perfect phrase for a poster—and eventually pulled his hair out in the attempt—recognizes that promotional writing is hard writing, and the fewer the words, the harder it is to find the right ones.

65 DISPLAY/ EXHIBIT MATERIALS	Display/exhibit materials epitomize one of freelancing's most crucial dictums: Never measure the worth of an assignment by the number of words it involves.

Get This Gig: Display/Exhibit Materials

Where Do I Start?

Visit the big-box or chain stores in your area and make note of how effective or ineffective their in-store displays are. Prepare a version of your introductory letter that refers specifically to display/exhibit writing as one aspect of the services you offer. For example, "The aim of my practice is to improve every piece of marketing or branding collateral, from in-store banners to elaborate product brochures." If you've noticed specific errors on any of the in-store materials, feel free to point them out as a way of bolstering your case, but make sure you avoid an inadvertently condescending tone.

Who Do I Contact?

Call the head offices of each of the companies whose stores you've visited and get the name of the marketing manager or vice president. Pop your letter in the mail to that person.

What Do I Charge?

As I said, it can take time even to find the right five words for a sticker. Just be sure not to charge so little that it looks as though you don't care what you get paid. Use the lawyer's approach here: Any project is worth at least an hour of your time.

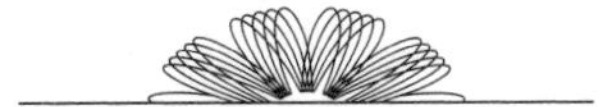

The Madness **OF WRITERS**

Often when I'm holed up in my office working on a new writing project, my wife Stephanie will walk in and ask me what I'm so excited about. I never actually realize that I'm acting excited, but she says she can always tell when I've found the story, by which she means I've finally corralled the structure, or the thread, for the piece I've been wrestling with. My whole demeanor changes, she says, as though I've stumbled upon a chest full of gold. She's right—I know no more ecstatic moment than the one in which the story crystallizes before me, sometimes after hours, days, or weeks of trying to find it. It's an instant of true magic for me—and one that utterly puzzles her, since the thought of taking a blank page and having to populate it with words is one she finds quite revolting.

"You're enjoying that, aren't you?" she'll say.

"More than I can tell you," I'll reply. Then she'll smile, shake her head, and walk out of the office as though she's just been talking to an alien. It's adorable, really.

 OUTLINES

At various turns called straw men, dot-dashes, storyboards, and a host of other names, the pieces belonging to this category, no matter what name they may go by in a company's particular vernacular, provide foundational frameworks from which to develop more complete versions—of project plans, presentations, documents, and so on. A straw man, for instance, is a preliminary business document intended to kick-start a broader discussion. A dot-dash is an outline consisting of key points and key subpoints around which to compose a complete document. A storyboard is a chronology of snapshots around which to craft a complete presentation. Each of these is highly effective when produced by someone skilled at articulating key ideas in a structured way. Someone like you.

An outline is the scaffolding on which the rest of the story is built.

Get This Gig: Outlines

Where Do I Start?

Outlines are all about imposing structure on content that would otherwise be loose and incoherent. So create a version of your introductory letter that emphasizes your ability to take any material, no matter how scattershot, and make of it a clear, compelling story that delivers all the relevant messages while being creative in presentation.

Who Do I Contact?

Marketing departments love writers who can pull together messages in tidy copy, thereby satisfying the demands of all the different internal stakeholders. Target the marketing manager.

What Do I Charge?

Outlines in all their forms can demand significant up-front time, so when providing your quote, remember to assume that extra 20 percent.

 NAMES

A good deal of my corporate work comes to me after others have tried their hand at seemingly easy writing tasks and failed. Quite often these tasks involve the need to name something—a new product, a line of products, a program or initiative, a proprietary concept or framework, even a company itself—and they're usually quite a bit of fun, since the process tends to be collaborative, intensive, and energizing. Plus, corporate naming isn't far removed from the creative writing process; it's only a stone's throw, in fact, from thinking of a title for your personal essay, a moniker for your protagonist, or a name for the fictional company in your short story. You're bringing to bear the same creative muscle and applying it to something that just happens to exist in the real world.

"You can't overstate the importance of an effective name."

—Kalina Marcysiak, Senior Business Transformation Consultant, IBM Global Business Services

Get This Gig: Names

Where Do I Start?

It's all about letting people know all the different ways a professional communicator can help. I actually scored my most recent naming gig because of this very book. I e-mailed a number of my corporate contacts asking if they'd be interested in offering quotes for various sections of the book. One of them e-mailed back saying, "I didn't know you do name brainstorming. We're desperately trying to find the right name for a hot new product we've developed. Can't get there. Think you could come in for two or three hours next week?" In your intro letter, whether your services are listed in paragraphs, as a bulleted list, or some other way, make sure you include a thorough sampling so that those receiving it will realize just how many ways there are in which you can be useful to them.

Who Do I Contact?

Freelance naming gigs will come mostly from Small Fish and Lone Wolves, since Big Dogs will have their in-house marketing teams handle it. Send your letter to the most senior people at as many of these organizations as you'd like.

What Do I Charge?

Charge by the hour, and don't skimp. Names are crucial in the business world. Your time spent helping figure them out is valuable.

TAGLINES/SLOGANS

A little further along the scale are the taglines/slogans needed to help sell the things you've helped name. And though the words contained in these pieces of mini-writing may come after the names themselves, they're hardly secondary. One could put up a pretty strong argument, in fact, that a tagline/slogan does more to sell the product or company than the name of the product or company itself. The word "Nike" could mean anything, but the three words "Just Do It" communicate an entire world of athletic endeavor and passion. "Raid" tells you virtually nothing; "Raid Kills Bugs Dead" tells you pretty much everything you need to know. Personally, I love these kinds of assignments because they're a terrific challenge and a tremendous opportunity to prove the true value of a professional writer. The fewer words one has to work with, the harder it is to amaze the reader—or, in this case, the client. Always have faith that, provided you put in the time, your talent will rise to the fore and create possibilities that cause the client to say, "Man, you're good."

68
TAGLINES/ SLOGANS

"A slogan may be just a few words, but it can speak volumes."

—Jennifer Ansley, Marketing Manager, Somerset Entertainment

Get This Gig: Taglines/Slogans

Where Do I Start?

Make sure your letter communicates the fact that writing is more than editing. Many people, until they find out otherwise, assume that freelance writers offer the corporate world little more than identification of erroneous commas. Yes, those bad commas drive me nuts, too, but the point here is to outline both levels of what you offer—standard writing and editing help plus communications expertise applicable to the entire range of marketing materials.

Who Do I Contact?

Marketing departments spend a huge number of hours trying to capture just the right words to describe a product or service. Send your letter to the marketing department head. Hopefully he will see the light and invite you in to make his job easier.

What Do I Charge?

You don't want to seem as though you don't know how long your own work takes you, so when you're asked to generate possible taglines/slogans, assume about a day's work for half a dozen good possibilities.

MISSION/VISION/VALUES STATEMENTS

A little further yet along the spectrum we find the sacrosanct words to which organizations religiously cleave: the mission/vision/values statements that let the rest of the world know why they exist, what they aim to be, and what's important to them.

It can be fashionable around the water cooler to joke that mission/vision/values statements are little more than fluff. But studies have shown that, when the employees of a company clearly understand its purpose and goals, better performance results. If a company is serious about its mission, vision, and values, you, as the person tapped to help pin them down, had better be serious about them, too; if nothing else, when you approach a writing assignment with a serious mindset, the writing is inevitably better.

To write these well, it's critical that you understand the distinctions among them. A mission statement describes the overall purpose and *raison d'être* of the organization ("To produce and sell ice cream."). A vision statement describes what the organization wants to become ("To be the number-one ice-cream-selling company in the Midwest."). Values (increasingly referred to today as "core values"—don't ask me why) are those traits the organization cares about and wishes to see reflected in its employees ("Superior Ice Cream values passion, integrity, commitment, and a complete and utter affection for ice cream in all its wonderful flavors."). Mission/vision/values statements are not meant to be fluid and dynamic over time; they are meant to be the philosophical bedrock on which the company operates. That means many people are going to have opinions about how the words contained in these statements should read, so be patient, open, collaborative, leave your ego at the door, and strive for something that will inspire pride and solidarity in everyone who reads them.

69 MISSION/ VISION/VALUES STATEMENTS	Mission/vision/values statements let the rest of the world know why a company exists, what it aims to be, and what it considers important.

Get This Gig: Mission/Vision/Values Statements

Where Do I Start?

Mission/vision/values statements are created to help publicize what a company is all about—its brand. Create a version of your introductory letter that includes clear mention of the help you can provide creating and refining brand communications.

Who Do I Contact?

Look up branding firms in your area and send your letter to their chief officers. Most of them will be Small Fish, so it's okay to target the top people.

What Do I Charge?

Mission/vision/values-type work is usually highly collaborative, involving meetings with many people in order to figure out what the organization truly stands for, what it wants to be, and what values it genuinely wishes to uphold. And then there's the actual writing part. When you get this kind of assignment, prepare a quote that assumes time for both research and writing.

QUESTIONNAIRES/SURVEYS

Companies base their strategies on what they can find out about their customers. They attempt lots of trickery to suss out this information, but there's one tried-and-true method they come back to again and again: the questionnaire/survey. I imagine you get hit with questionnaires/surveys all the time, these days mostly online. Sometimes, if you're feeling generous, you even fill them out.

Questionnaires/surveys are the easiest, most direct way to gather information, but for them to achieve their aim, they need to be properly written. You may not think of a questionnaire/survey as something that can be written well or poorly, but please believe me when I tell you that *anything* can be written well or poorly. A questionnaire/survey is a superb example of this. Those that are written poorly will contain vague questions, an indistinct structure, and a sense of overlap throughout—that the questionnaire/survey steps on its own feet. Questionnaire/surveys that accomplish their objectives do so because they contain questions that are both clear and nonthreatening, allowing the recipient to answer without feeling confused, misdirected, or ill at ease.

The same goes for internal questionnaires/surveys, used often by companies to take the pulse of its staff. Such questionnaires/surveys can hardly be put together willy-nilly; they need to extract highly specific answers in a highly sensitive way. If handed such an assignment, you need to ask many questions yourself before writing the questions for others. When was the last time a questionnaire/survey was sent out? What were the results like? Did people have trouble answering any of the questions in particular? What are the most important pieces of information you're trying to draw out? Are there any specific sensitivities you're aware of among the recipient group?

70 QUESTIONNAIRES/ SURVEYS	Questionnaires/surveys that achieve their objectives do so because they're clear and nonthreatening.

Get This Gig: Questionnaires/Surveys

Where Do I Start?

Create a version of your blanket letter that spotlights questionnaires/surveys as perfect examples of what you do. ("Focused, effective questionnaires and surveys are just one of the services I provide.") Mention the other stuff, too, but put these up front so anyone with that particular need won't have a chance to miss it.

Who Do I Contact?

Questionnaires/surveys are usually marshaled by human resources departments and employed primarily by Big Dogs with the marketing budgets to accommodate them. Aim for the large firms, and get your letter into the hands of their human resources managers.

What Do I Charge?

As with mission/vision/values statements, try to determine as accurately as possible how much nonwriting work you'll have to do—I'm talking about meetings, reviewing material, and research—and then, in your quote, split out that part of the assignment from the writing part so it's clear how you're calculating the estimated hours.

 HUMAN RESOURCES MATERIALS

As a company's main storehouse of employee information, operational principles, and specific protocols, every human resources department is by necessity document-heavy. The organization's silent eyes and ears, often exerting more control from behind the scenes than is apparent, Human Resources, more than any other area, needs to have things officially recorded, from job postings to expense guidelines to staff evaluations. This translates into lots of stuff being written down, and people needed to write it. Because human resources documents are so critical, they need to be done exactly right, so those in charge often turn to writers to capture that special balance of thoroughness and concision that so many find elusive.

71 HUMAN RESOURCES MATERIALS	"It's paramount that human resources documents are clear, thorough, and effective. They're the company's foundation." —Mara Gunner, Human Resources and Organizational Development, Royal Ontario Museum

Get This Gig: Human Resources Materials

Where Do I Start?

Ask friends of yours employed at Big Dogs or Small Fish to swipe some human resources materials from work; then use those types of materials as examples to cite in your introductory letter. Communicate the fact that you understand human resources materials need to be clear, thorough, and accurate—exactly the principles your practice is based on.

Who Do I Contact?

Send the letter to human resources managers at as many Big Dogs and Small Fish as you feel like targeting.

What Do I Charge?

Human resources materials aren't that far removed from legal documents insofar as they often must include highly specific information. So be prepared to go back and forth multiple times on documents that appear relatively straightforward. The way I get around this is by building two rounds of feedback and revision into my initial quote. I make it clear to the client that, beyond those two rounds, the meter starts running.

AWARD NOMINATIONS

Most every company has some type of program whereby employees can be nominated and acknowledged for standout performance within a particular context—on a specific project, say, or for exhibiting bang-up customer service, or for doing exemplary work over the course of a month, or for finding a creative solution to a pressing issue. It usually falls to supervisors or managers to complete such nominations (and submit them to Human Resources, of course), but these people are, ironically, often those with the least time in which to do so, so typically they're only too happy to hand off the responsibility to someone else—someone who can work within the parameters of a standard nomination template, or within the nonparameters of no template at all, and forcefully communicate why a certain accomplishment, by a certain person, merits recognition.

72 AWARD NOMINATIONS	Studies have shown that the number-one thing people want at work isn't a bigger salary or extra status, but recognition for their efforts. Awards go a long way toward achieving that goal.

Get This Gig: Award Nominations

Where Do I Start?

The more proprietary materials or templates you develop, the better chance you have of getting your foot in the corporate door. Ask friends and associates if they can provide you samples of the award nomination templates and forms used by their companies, then see if you can't dream up some original but professional-looking forms a human resources manager might want to implement.

Who Do I Contact?

The larger the organization, the more likely it is to have a formalized award or recognition program and materials to support it. So it makes the most sense to target human resources managers at Big Dogs as a starting point.

What Do I Charge?

If people are interested in your writing award-related content according to their existing materials, charge by the hour. If they're interested in using materials you've created, you can charge them a licensing or rights fee. The size of this fee depends on a few factors, including how extensive the materials are and how big the company is, but a few thousand dollars is usually the right neighborhood. It's best to ask the advice of a corporate lawyer should you find yourself in this situation.

CATALOGS

Companies that sell stuff need to let their customers know what kinds of things they sell, how much they sell them for, and how they can be purchased. This is done in countless ways today—online stores, banner ads, leaflets, e-mail blitzes—but the most time-honored method is still the good old-fashioned catalog. From IKEA to Victoria's Secret to Pottery Barn, companies still rely on catalogs to sell their products as much as they do any other channel, and those catalogs still have the same mix of content as they did a century ago: appealing photos, brief descriptions of most of the products, longer descriptions of a few featured ones, prices, and order forms. Some catalogs contain extensive writing. The catalog produced by clothing company Coldwater Creek, for example, includes almost an entire story for every item it shows.

Because of the intense competition for consumer dollars today, companies know that a single typo or mismatched caption in a catalog could mean loss of customers, so they ensure that the words going into that catalog are put through multiple drafts and scrutinized by numerous sets of eyes before seeing the light of day. Often they'll seek someone from outside the company to bring an objective view to the catalog content, and a writer is exactly the kind of person they'll seek.

The extent of what you're asked to do will depend on the stage at which you're brought in. If toward the end of the project, you'll typically be asked to do a thorough proofread of the copy. If you're brought in closer to the beginning, you might be given leeway to make editorial suggestions or, if right at the outset, recommendations to the overall layout and structure. In the end, catalogs are a bit like annual reports: Though they aren't quite showcases for your creative gifts, they probably represent bigger opportunities than you think. To you, fixing some erratic punctuation, putting a few quotation marks where they belong, and altering a handful of clunky phrases doesn't seem like a big deal. It might even feel boring. But to the marketing vice president who's been put in charge of getting a flawless catalog out the door, a guy who's utterly swamped but still needs to get this right, your work is not only impressive—it matters. In a big way.

73
CATALOGS

Companies still rely on catalogs to sell their products. And it isn't just the pictures that sell the products—it's the words.

Get This Gig: Catalogs

Where Do I Start?

Go through every catalog you receive to get a feel for the kind of writing it contains. Look for errors or places where you think the copy could be stronger. You're not trying to throw anyone under the bus here; you're just making the subtle suggestion that you might be able to do a superior job with the same material. Create a version of your introductory letter that makes specific reference to that company's catalog. Tailor it specifically for each company you target.

Who Do I Contact?

Send your letter to the marketing manager, since it's her department that's responsible for turning out the catalog. Try to time it so your letter is received six months before the catalog comes out, since that's about the time production on it will begin.

What Do I Charge?

Estimate your hours by asking exactly which parts of the catalog you're being asked to edit or write. You might be required to edit fifty two-sentence captions or to compose the customer letter on the inside cover. Get a clear idea of (a) what you're working on, and (b) what proportion is writing vs. editing, then determine your quote.

LETTERS

All companies write to their customers. The bigger the company, the more letters they send. My biggest corporate assignment in the past year came from a Big Dog financial client for whom I'd been editing some product campaign brochures. One afternoon the vice president of marketing approached me and said, "Our customer letters are shit. Can you help?" "Of course," I replied. (Remember: You can *always* help.) I asked how many different letters there were. "About three hundred, I think," he said. "Or maybe five hundred, I'm not sure." This brief exchange led to my reviewing and revising all of those letters. I didn't want to see any financial letters for a while after that, but it was certainly a nice assignment to get.

74 LETTERS	Many companies try to save money by asking their marketers to be writers, too. Then they find out the two skills are very different. That's where you come in.

Get This Gig: Letters

Where Do I Start?

Prepare a version of your intro letter that talks strictly about the importance of effective customer communications (you can even say "customer-facing" communications if it turns your fancy) and how well you understand that importance. List a number of different types of such communications, including brochures, flyers, company Web sites, and, most important of all, letters. You're positioning yourself as an expert at helping companies talk to their customers.

Who Do I Contact?

Keeping the letters you receive in the mail for just a week or two will give you plenty of prospects to target. Remember, don't send your letter to the head of Communications; send it to the head of Marketing. Whenever possible, gently point out errors in the letters you've received from the company or offer a handful of specific suggestions for improvement. They just might be swayed by the fact that you've spotted things their own people didn't.

What Do I Charge?

Customer letters are delicate animals, so they do take time. Use the standard guideline—an hour for every 250 words of writing or 500 words of editing—but be prepared for it to expand if necessary.

ADVERTISEMENTS

Advertising can take diverse forms, including billboards or posters, print ads in magazines, radio or TV spots, and direct mail pieces. A fair chunk of most companies' budgets are devoted to advertising (subsumed within the overall marketing budget), so the copy that goes into those ads must be precise and strategic.

Though both companies and customers understand that the sole purpose of an ad is for the former to try to sell something to the latter, they maintain a tacit understanding that heavy-handed, in-your-face ads are unwelcome. Ad copy must therefore arouse customers' interest and stir them to action while not seeming to do so. This is a subtle trick, one that you, as a professional writer, can perform better than anyone.

As you do more and more work for a company, you may find yourself being asked to participate in advertising work that goes beyond strict copywriting. Creative types are usually creative in more than one way, and once you're recognized as an "idea" person in general, don't be surprised if your clients ask you to help with things like general concept work on campaigns, brainstorming on specific ads, even graphic and layout composition. After a few months producing a departmental newsletter at Procter & Gamble, I was approached one morning by a junior associate named Chris whom I'd gotten to know fairly well but with whom I hadn't worked directly. He pulled me into a boardroom with a dozen other people, closed the lights, and popped in a videocassette. Suddenly a commercial for Folgers coffee came on, featuring the addictive jingle, "The best part of waking up is Folgers in your cup." Chris then turned the lights back on and asked everyone, including me, what they thought of the commercial, which was to hit stations the following week. At first I was surprised to have been brought in, but then I realized why it had made perfect sense to Chris. This was creative work that involved communicating with customers. It's the kind of thing likely to happen to you, too: Those you work for, and with, will open your eyes to areas that fall quite naturally within your range of expertise but that you never thought about pursuing before. Those people deserve your thanks, because once you add a new wrinkle to your range of services, it's there for good—and every extra wrinkle is another potential way in the door.

75 ADVERTISEMENTS	It doesn't matter whether companies want to advertise. They have to. And they know that both the images and the words have to be just right.

Get This Gig: Advertisements

Where Do I Start?

Big Dogs' marketing departments use dedicated in-house copywriters to give life to the ads they produce. But at Small Fish, even when people are hired for one role, they often end up doing many. Hold on to that steady avalanche of ads you get in the mail every week, and make a list of the companies who send them. Then create a version of your introductory letter that specifically highlights your interest and expertise in copywriting (which is the same as ad writing).

Who Do I Contact?

Call the Small Fish on your list and get the names of their marketing managers. Send your letter to them. You can try the Big Dogs, too, but they'll be looking specifically for copywriters, so in the letter you should call yourself one.

What Do I Charge?

When writing ad copy you usually need to meet with graphic designers, the project manager, and others working on the same piece. Ascertain all these needs in your initial meeting, then prepare an appropriate quote using the standard guideline of an hour per 250 words of writing or 500 words of editing.

ADVERTORIALS

The word *advertorial* comes from the blend of advertisement and editorial; it's intended to stir customer interest under the guise of sharing expertise or knowledge from a particular point of view. An insurance company, for example, might pay to have an insert included in a business magazine in which they outline the slam-dunk advantages of life insurance. Oh, and by the way, they just happen to offer a bunch of different types of insurance, too. The piece takes the appearance of an editorial, but its purpose is to sell the company's products or services by presenting an argument that, directly or indirectly, endorses the benefits.

76 ADVERTORIALS	An advertorial is halfway between an ad and an editorial—it uses expertise and a specific viewpoint to pique customer interest.

Get This Gig: Advertorials

Where Do I Start?

Educate yourself on the difference between advertisements and advertorials. Look at several examples of both and see what they're trying to accomplish and the respective ways in which they go about doing so. Clearly mention both types of writing in your introductory letter.

Who Do I Contact?

Advertorials aren't cheap, so the majority of them come from Big Dogs and, to a lesser extent, Small Fish. The marketing department produces them; send your introductory letter to the top marketing contact you can find at these companies.

What Do I Charge?

An hour for every 250 words of writing or 500 words of editing.

FOCUS-GROUP INPUT

To help determine whether a certain product or service will be enthusiastically received in the marketplace, companies will sometimes go straight to the source, real-life consumers. They gather customers in a room with a facilitator, feed them pastries and coffee, and have them answer a number of sneaky questions so they'll reveal exactly what the company wants to know—thereby justifying the investment of conducting the group since they stand to make millions extra as a result of the information it produces.

The key to these sessions, of course, is asking good questions, getting people talking, and accurately recording the results to report back to the company. Don't be shocked if one of your clients asks if you'd be interested in facilitating one of these sessions. The way they see it, you're a professional communicator, and who better to lead an exercise in which the most important traits are articulateness, coherence, a feel for dialogue, the ability to quickly process and interpret what people are saying in order to squeeze as much information out of them as possible—and, as I said, a knack for capturing the most salient parts of an extensive discussion in a clear, meaningful way.

Consumer focus groups aren't the only type. You might be asked to conduct the same type of session internally, with a selection of the organization's employees, to help paint a representative picture of the staff's general frame of mind, including specific praise or grievances. I said earlier that internal surveys are often used by an organization to take the pulse of its staff. Sometimes the organization's senior brass choose to bypass this step and take the more direct route of talking to its people in a live setting. That is, having *you* talk to its people in a live setting.

You might also be asked to conduct a session with a sampling of staff from one of the company's clients. I am surprised at how few companies do this, since I've always seen it translate into a higher success rate and an improved supplier-client relationship. Occasionally I've been asked to conduct these sessions, and I've found them enjoyable.

First, since I don't represent the company directly, I'm not seen as a threat, so people talk more freely. Second, meeting new people means making more contacts. Finally, since the organization is depending on me to come back with information it can use, I have to be on from the get-go, and I appreciate both the challenge as well as the opportunity to use my communications skills in a creative way.

77 FOCUS-GROUP INPUT	Why do writers make good focus-group facilitators? Because they know how to ask good questions, and they know how to report the answers.

Get This Gig: Focus-Group Input

Where Do I Start?

Group facilitation is perceived as a distinct skill, so you need to either develop a specific letter that showcases it, or, if you prefer, to give it an unmistakable shout-out in your customary note.

Who Do I Contact?

Focus groups are run by companies of every type for all the different reasons mentioned above. They are usually coordinated by Marketing in conjunction with Human Resources, who act more as watchdogs to the process. Rather than wasting time and postage, call the companies you're curious about and ask them directly if they ever conduct focus groups. When the person on the other end asks why, say because you're an experienced focus-group facilitator and you'd like to send an introductory letter to the appropriate person outlining the potential benefits. With a polished answer like that, how could they not give you the information?

What Do I Charge?

Charge an hourly rate, and make sure to include the time you spend preparing, the time you spend in the session itself, and the time you spend consolidating and reporting the input.

BUSINESS CASES

When a department or a team wants to propose a project, initiative, or program, they typically need to justify it to the company's decision makers with a well-considered business case. The business case lays out the rationale for the project using explanations, figures, comparisons, analyses, assumptions, and, finally, projections. Since they are among the most tightly structured of business documents, business cases benefit from the talents of those who can wield different elements—prose, tables, graphs, charts, and so on—to tell a persuasive story.

At a minimum, the business case will provide some background or context, the reason for doing the project now, the expected costs, the expected risks, and the envisioned results and benefits. More detailed business cases may include in-depth market analyses, interdependencies with other departments, key stakeholders, the proposed project team and project sponsor, expected resource requirements, a preliminary critical path, and a boatload of other stuff.

Remember that no matter the length or format of a business case, its purpose is always the same: to convince those with the power to give the thumbs-up that this project makes sense for the company, now. Keep in mind also that since business cases are usually presented to senior people who have incredibly busy schedules, they need to be succinct, straightforward, and crystal clear about what they are proposing.

78
BUSINESS CASES

"A business case should be watertight—but it had also better sound good."

—Beatrix Dart, Associate Dean, Executive Degree Programs, Executive Director, Initiatives for Women in Business, and Professor of Strategic Management, Rotman School of Management, University of Toronto

Get This Gig: Business Cases

Where Do I Start?

Go to the nearest bookstore, grab a book like *The Ten-Day MBA* by Steven Silbiger or *Complete MBA for Dummies* by Kathleen Allen, PhD and Peter Economy off the shelf, and flip to the section on business cases. Study how they're laid out, their components, their format, and the way they're constructed to make a persuasive argument. In your introductory letter, note business cases as one of your particular areas of specialization, and perhaps one of your first-time discount or pro bono categories. For example, you might tag business cases, white papers, and speeches as items that, for first-time clients, you'll write for free as long as they come in under ten hours, or some other total you feel is appropriate. It's a great way to hook clients.

Who Do I Contact?

Any department trying to get a project approved might generate a business case, but Human Resources will in general disseminate information about freelancers or vendors of interest to the rest of the company—so send your letter to the human resources manager, including mention of business cases as part of the services you offer.

What Do I Charge?

Assembling a business case will require that you solicit input from various departments, including Finance, Product Development, and Marketing. When determining your quote, ask questions to determine how much time you'll likely need to spend on that part of the work. Then add 20 percent.

SCENARIOS/HYPOTHETICALS

Because they are built around figures, numbers, and projections, business cases are by definition fairly dry reading. Related to them, however, are documents that bolster the business case rationale by painting a picture based on present facts or future assumptions. The former type is typically used to depict the collective behavior of a particular type of customer in order to better understand its needs. The latter is often used to develop a portrait of a specific customer group in order to market to them as effectively as possible. Here's an example: A financial client of mine, analyzing demographic projections for the next decade, realized it needed specific strategies to market its services to two emerging groups in particular: working moms, a group that would continue to grow, and Zoomers, the older kids of baby boomers, who were still in the midst of defining themselves and in the meantime consuming everything in sight, from technology to chai lattés.

The company brought me aboard to take the work done by its research team and turn it into concrete scenarios—a day in the life of each group, if you will. I loved this assignment, because it essentially involved writing a story, with the characters and their backgrounds and desires handed to me on a silver platter. Based on the stories I wrote, the company built strategic marketing plans to go after each group. And you thought there was no room for creative writing in the corporate world.

79 SCENARIOS/ HYPOTHETICALS	Based on future assumptions, scenarios/hypotheticals are often used to develop a portrait of a particular customer group in order to market to them as effectively as possible.

Get This Gig: Scenarios/Hypotheticals

Where Do I Start?

Google "customer segment analysis," "consumer demographics," and any other related phrases you can come up with. Read some of the articles these searches generate—they'll show you the kind of data companies use to create scenarios/hypotheticals and, consequently, to make certain gambles. Get to understand the behaviors and habits of each customer segment or group, and familiarize yourself with the ways in which each group is shrinking, growing, or changing. Then create a version of your letter that specifically points up the scenario-generating part of your practice, in which you take existing data and use it to craft future scenarios around which marketing departments can noodle crucial decisions for the future.

Who Do I Contact?

The bigger the company, the more likely they'll have an appetite for this kind of service. Big Dogs in particular are willing to entertain this type of investment, because the people who work for them are always trying to introduce different, memorable elements. Send your letter to the marketing manager and follow up by phone after a few weeks.

What Do I Charge?

A scenario/hypothetical will often take the form of a story. Either bill a total number of hours at the end of the project or determine an estimate based on (a) how long you believe it will take you to write the scenario/hypothetical, and (b) how many hours you think you'll need for research such as examining data, reading reports, and talking to different staff.

PROSPECTUSES

Also related to business cases, but more creative in execution, are prospectuses: documents that describe the major features of proposed projects or ventures in enough detail that prospective patrons, clients, participants, or investors can make sound decisions regarding their potential involvement. A prospectus can be written for just about anything, from a restaurant to a hedge fund, and, like scenarios/hypotheticals, they consist mostly of prose, rather than data, which makes them pretty fun to write. Say you want to open a bagel store in New Haven, Connecticut. The business case you present to investors would provide the financial details—your overhead, your taxes, your expected revenue, and so on—but the prospectus would tell the in-depth story behind the idea, too—why the people of New Haven would be expected to flock to a bagel store, why the temperature patterns in the city mean people are out on a Saturday morning more often than not, how the store would follow successful models opened elsewhere in the region. It's still a business document talking about business ideas, but above all it's a story, and that story must be compelling in the eyes of those deciding whether to, literally, buy into it. Potential investors can look at assumptions and projections all day, but in the end these are still guesses. What persuades someone toward a certain course of action? A great story. You know it, I know it, and businesses know it, too.

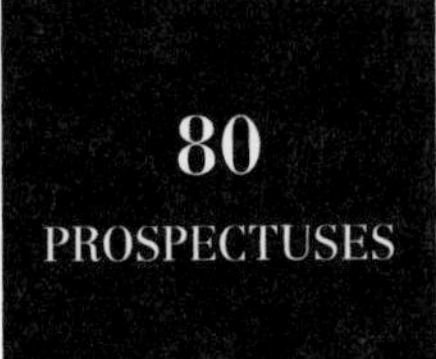

A prospectus is a document describing a business idea in a persuasive way in order to convince potential investors and other stakeholders of its promise. But above all, it's a story.

Get This Gig: Prospectuses

Where Do I Start?

Read several prospectuses to understand how they're distinct from proposals (for more on that, see the following section) and business cases. In your standard letter, mention all three.

Who Do I Contact?

Send your letter to both the human resources manager and marketing manager. Big Dogs, Small Fish, and Lone Wolves all might have reason to produce prospectuses for one reason or another, so don't exclude any of them.

What Do I Charge?

Like business cases, prospectuses will demand that you pull together lots of information from disparate sources. That's likely to occupy a fair chunk of hours. The best thing you can do for both yourself and your client is to establish mutual clarity from the get-go, after which you can deliver an estimate you're confident in.

PROPOSALS

Related to prospectuses, which are usually created to provide information to investors, are proposals, which are usually created for the unadulterated purpose of asking directly for something, most often business.

Business cases lay out inclusive, tightly structured financial projections and analyses, targeting the audience's wallet via its brain. Proposals might target the wallet, too, but they're just as likely to go through the heart or some other creative path. Business cases rationalize a course of action that will benefit the company in some way—case closed. Proposals are much more varied depending on both the company creating them and the audience they're being created for. I once wrote two separate proposals for a real estate brokerage firm wanting to represent first an upscale hotel chain and, second, Planet Hollywood. You can imagine how different those two proposals looked.

All proposals, no matter how they're packaged, share a basic structure. They must explain the audience's specific need, articulate the proposed solution, lay out its specific advantages, and describe why it's better than any other alternatives.

The most important thing to remember when writing a business proposal is this: Focus not on the company doing the proposing but on the audience it's proposing to.

Get This Gig: Proposals

Where Do I Start?

Surf the Web for proposals of different types—real estate proposals, financial proposals, marketing proposals, business proposals ... everything short of marriage proposals. Learn about the various forms they come in and the ingredients they're usually composed of. Judge them on the effectiveness with which they tell a convincing story. Peruse a copy of *Writing Winning Business Proposals* by Richard C. Freed, Shervin Freed, and Joe Romano. Then, since Big Dogs, Small Fish, and Lone Wolves all have occasion to bid for projects, make proposal writing a conspicuous part of your standard letter.

Who Do I Contact?

The marketing manager. In almost every case, the proposal is at some point going to end up in Marketing's hands.

What Do I Charge?

Proposals can be difficult to quote on because of the extensive thinking time they often require. That is, outside of the actual content writing, you might spend a great deal of time mentally storyboarding, revising the structure, adding here, removing there, and dummying in placeholders to be completed later. As always, ask for as much information up front as possible on which to base your estimate. As a default, use a rate of an hour and a half per page or PowerPoint slide.

TIMELINES/CRITICAL PATHS

Though I'm a writer, I've spent a lot of time in different offices, around a range of clients, and on various project teams—and I can tell you there's isn't a project in the world that doesn't run better when it's organized around a specific, documented timeline/critical path that has specific owners accountable for the deliverables and milestones built into it. Yes, that was a cringe-inducing bit of corporate-speak I just laid on you, but those buzzwords do sometimes have their place. Anyone who has tried to manage a strategic initiative or multifaceted project plan without a timeline/critical path to keep it focused can well understand how much better things run when there *is* a plan in place.

Why are writers naturally good at developing timelines/critical paths? Because they're used to visualizing the entire story.

Get This Gig: Timelines/Critical Paths

Where Do I Start?

Google "critical path"—lots of stuff will come up that demonstrates a solid, sound way to create a project timeline/critical path. This type of work involves project management as well as raw writing, but think of it as keeping multiple characters on track as you stalk the finish line of a story. If you're inclined, research as many timeline/critical path-type forms and templates as you can, then create some proprietary ones of your own that you can mention in your standard letter or announce via a more customized one.

Who Do I Contact?

Though every department in a company can benefit from good project management tools, make the marketing manager your initial target, since that's the area (not counting Communications) to which your skill set is most closely matched.

What Do I Charge?

If you're getting in on the ground floor of a project and being asked to adapt some existing materials, make a fair estimate according to an hourly rate. If a company is asking to use materials you've created, charge a licensing fee. (See Award Nominations on page 153.)

WEB COPY

Last in this section, but hardly least in today's world, is online writing. Since most people today make the Internet their first step when wanting to learn more about, well, anything, it stands to reason that what companies place on their Web sites is as important as, if not more important than, what they put in print. Almost any professional freelancer will report an increase in the proportion of Web writing they've been requested to do over the past several years. Company Web sites are no longer side projects meant to supplement print material. They are full-scale, ongoing endeavors often maintained by an entire team or occupying their own department. Since most organizations are increasing their Web content out of necessity but not correspondingly reducing their print output, the volume of stuff they need written has ballooned. This is great news for you.

Keep in mind that Web writing isn't the same as writing for print. People are less patient online, so Web copy usually needs to be shorter, more concise, and, for the purposes of visual ease, more broken up. Showing you can tell the same story with equal impact in print and online will help solidify your status as an indispensable resource.

83 WEB COPY	"A company's Web site is its calling card. If it doesn't sound good, you're in trouble." —Martin Traub-Werner, Vice President, Raybec Communications

Get This Gig: Web Copy

Where Do I Start?

Simple—start surfing, baby. The Web is your oyster. Visit as many sites as you want, making notes about what works and what doesn't, recording errors big and small, perhaps printing out sample pages and marking them with suggested changes. One thing will become clear to you during this exercise: There's enough bad Web writing out there to make you feel good. For companies whose Web sites have the most errors or contain the poorest writing, customize a version of your introductory letter that points out, using real examples, the kinds of ways in which you might be able to help them present the company more effectively. As always, be sure to do this with a kind, helpful, collaborative tone, not one that's in any way patronizing or arrogant.

Who Do I Contact?

Big Dogs, Small Fish, and Lone Wolves all have Web sites, and they all rely on them increasingly to drive customer interest and activity.

Send your letter to one of them, ten of them, a hundred, or until your envelopes run out.

What Do I Charge?

When quoting on Web writing, use the same rule of thumb as you do for print: an hour of your time for every 250 words of writing or every 500 words of editing.

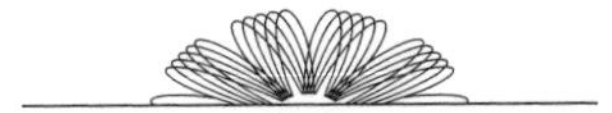

Spell-Check Your E-Mails (AND DON'T STOP THERE)

As a professional writer, you're justifiably held to a higher standard of communication even in casual correspondence. While others can get away with messages characterized by endless emoticons and stomach-turning grammar, you can't. Before you send that three-line e-mail to the editor with whom you're just touching base, do a spell-check. Ninety-nine times out of a hundred, you won't find anything, but the one mistake you catch might make or break a pivotal relationship. And if you're truly serious about ensuring a professional image, don't stop at the spell-check. Go through your messages word by word, even letter by letter, to make sure no homonyms have slipped by that might alter things irredeemably. Your first instinct may tell you it isn't worth the time to do this, but keep in mind that the next writer, or the one after that, *is* going to take the time, and bypassing that extra step means giving him an unnecessary edge. Worse, your error might be immortalized, like the unfortunate writer whose story describing a man who had "lapsed into a comma" found its way to the desk of *The Washington Post* Copy Chief Bill Walsh, who used the gaffe as part of the title of his editors' and writers' guide, *Lapsing Into a Comma: A Curmudgeon's Guide to the Many Things That Can Go Wrong in Print—and How to Avoid Them*. Nor do you want to suffer the fate of Walsh's brother, who, while at PR Newswire, inadvertently sent out a Goldman Sachs press release referring to the firm, regrettably for him, as Goddamn Sacks.

EVERYTHING ELSE UNDER THE SUN

Like most teenagers, I was a regular visitor to McDonald's. In fact, if I think about it long enough, it's pretty scary just how often I patronized the golden arches, and just how quickly I devoured those Quarter Pounders.

I was also a proud employee of the megalith chain for a glorious six months during the summer of my fifteenth year. While furtively downing boxes of McNuggets in the storage room, I would often read the copy on the tray liners, marveling at how frequently they were rotated. I'd also think about who wrote them. Was it someone at Head Office with a bit of downtime? A guest writer who'd swagger in like Sinatra in a studio, toss down the copy, and swagger back out? A team of writers with papers crumpled in their fists shouting at each other about precisely what should be said regarding hotcakes and sausages?

Though I was never again able to wear the shoes I used while employed at McDonald's—I worked in the kitchen—my time there was still extremely valuable, given that you can't put a price on free McNuggets. What I couldn't have predicted was that my McDonald's experience would come full circle twenty years later. Here's what happened. A freelance writer with a slowly-but-surely growing practice, I'd developed a solid association with a guy who coached companies on their brand focus and consistency. He would kindly look for opportunities to throw a few bucks my way when it was appropriate for me to help write brand-related copy for his clients. I'd bust my hump on these assignments both to repay his generosity and to try to generate referrals.

One of these referrals, originally a direct client of the brand coach, ended up moving on to a big ad agency that served A-list companies across North America. This guy asked me to write a speech for the executive to whom he reported when that executive was on the hook for delivering the keynote at a big gala thrown by one of the agency's biggest clients. Because the speech made an impact, someone else at the agency asked for my name and contacted me to ask if I'd like to work on the account he was about to take over: McDonald's. What were they looking for? I asked. They're about to push a new "Chicken Choices" campaign, he said, and they needed someone to research and write three different tray liners to support it. The project turned out to be equal parts challenging, stimulating, and rewarding, to say nothing of the importance of adding a client of that stature to my résumé.

The longer I write, the more I'm surprised by the frequency with which work comes to me from unexpected sources or in unexpected ways. I don't know of any other career that allows one to become knowledgeable in so many different areas, gain access to such a diverse set of people, or bear witness to so many different types of products or outcomes that are at least partially a result of your contribution. It often seems as though for every magazine article I'm assigned or corporate assignment I earn, some new writing project lands in my lap from an unforeseen corner. And, while the magazine articles and corporate assignments are all wonderful in their own way, it's the stuff I don't see coming that usually proves most memorable.

The Landscape

One of the best parts about being a freelance writer is discovering just how often people have writing needs they'd rather have handled by someone else. Typically these projects don't belong in any formal publishing category, though taking them on can enhance your career in manifold ways. I sometimes feel as though I've written just about everything for people over the years, but every time I have this thought, something new comes my way. Attempting to define the landscape for all the miscellaneous writing projects that exist is in many ways an unfair exercise, since the possibilities are virtually limitless. Instead, let's just talk about some of the different requests you might encounter as you spread your writing wings ever wider.

RÉSUMÉS

Résumés, also called CVs (from the Latin *curriculum vitae*), are the essential tool in anyone's potential-employment bag. Companies differ greatly in their hiring methods and criteria, but every one of them asks for a résumé, because that's how they find out where you've worked, what you've done, and where you learned to speak all those languages.

When someone asks you to work on his résumé, keep a few things in mind.

First, it's going to take twice as long as you think—to make it good, at least. Most people's résumés contain dull, dry, passive language that reads more like the phone book than a document meant to intrigue a potential employer. The average résumé also lays out a laundry list of standard points explaining a person's duties in their previous roles, when what employers actually want to see are examples that show (a) the person takes initiative, (b) the person gets results, and (c) the person takes on challenges. Altering language in this way isn't easy, and it isn't quick. Often it requires lengthy conversations with the person in question to draw out the information that will give the résumé the substance and pop it needs.

Second, people tend to want to cram everything they can into their job history, but take me at my word when I tell you no résumé needs to be more than two pages long. Think of it this way: If someone has three pages' worth of impressive job experience, the first two pages of that experience are representative and impressive enough not to need the third.

Finally, to craft the best résumé you can for someone, keep in mind that you aren't just presenting a random set of points; you're telling a story.

84

RÉSUMÉS

In anyone's potential-employment bag, résumés are the essential tool.

Get This Gig: Résumés

Where Do I Start?

In your marketing materials, call out résumé work clearly—it can be a regular hit, since there are always people looking for jobs, and always resumes crying out for improvement.

Who Do I Contact?

Everyone in your personal database. I once had a bank executive I'd worked for on a contract ask me to work on his wife's résumé after she was laid off.

What Do I Charge?

As I said, résumés should be kept to two pages, but they usually require considerable work. It depends on whether you just need to tighten some bullet-point language or give the thing a complete overhaul. Between one and five hours' work is usually appropriate.

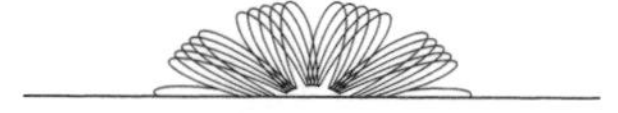

Riding the RÉSUMÉ

Shel Horowitz, freelancer, Hadley, Massachusetts

Back in 1981, I started my business originally as a typing service. My intention was to run it until my freelance magazine/newspaper career took off. Early on, clients started asking if I could help with their résumés. As it happened, I had struggled with my own résumé, encompassing seven different career paths, short job histories, and other challenges, and had a pretty good handle on how to package people's best virtues to prospective employers. I began actively seeking résumé work, and it was my primary source of income for ten years. And that was good, because the typing work dried up as computers became popular. I still write résumés today, when asked, but other parts of my business have replaced it as the primary income stream. Oh, yes, and one of my résumé clients landed a job as founding director of a university Family Business Center. He asked me if I would cover his conferences for his newsletter, and for the next fourteen years, I had a steady gig writing conference coverage for him, about twelve articles a year. For the ten years that followed the résumé stint, I focused on writing marketing materials for authors and publishers, small businesses, and nonprofits. This in turn evolved into book shepherding, which typically has a large writing component to it. For example, I have a recent client with a memoir, and I wrote her a letter that got her noticed by Paramount Pictures. I'm currently writing three articles for another client who originally came to me for consulting on book publishing and marketing.

WEDDING SPEECHES

Most wedding speeches one hears are interchangeable with any other wedding speech one hears, because they're typically filled with generic descriptions, clichéd metaphors, or empty platitudes. A professional's touch can make a wedding toast memorable instead of forgettable.

I've been asked to help with a number of wedding toasts over the years—by best men, maids of honor, grooms, brides, parents of the bride and groom, and friends asked to speak—and I've been tickled by each request, because I consider such assignments particularly special. After all, the words one delivers on his or her wedding day are frozen in time—not to mention heard by, sometimes, several hundred people. Wedding speeches can be slippery animals for a writer because they're going to be written by you but delivered by someone else, and that someone else has to make the words you've written sound spontaneous and sincere.

No matter who approaches you, simply get them talking so you can get past the ordinary stuff and find the depth and originality in their particular relationship. For instance, when grooms come to me for help, they'll have often scribbled down thoughts such as "There are no words to express how much I love you" or "You're so beautiful outside and in." I'll take him out for lunch and start asking questions—about his bride, when they met, the things that make her special, his parents, his friends, his passions. Then I think about where the true meat of the story lies, just as I would if I were drafting branding copy for a client. His saying he loves her because "she's so funny," for example, doesn't qualify. What makes her funny? Does she giggle in her sleep? Is she endearingly klutzy? Does she compose limericks on the spot? Similarly, saying he finds her "the most beautiful girl in the world" counts for zippo. Which of her features really does it for him? Do her eyes freeze him in place? Is it that charming smirk that sometimes only he notices? Is it that irresistible spot on the small of her back? No matter who you're helping, get specific, and remember that you aren't just laying out thoughts—you're telling a story.

The words delivered at a wedding are frozen in time. You can help make sure they age beautifully.

Get This Gig: Wedding Speeches

Where Do I Start?

First, draw attention to this part of your practice in the marketing materials you use. Second, whenever you're around an engaged couple, casually mention to the groom in private that part of your work is speechwriting, and you'd be happy to offer your help if he's interested. Yes, I know you hate doing that sort of thing, but if you're going to be a professional writer, you're going to have to tell people about the stuff you write. Trust me, they'll appreciate knowing.

Who Do I Contact?

Who speaks at a wedding is driven by numerous factors, including culture, religion, geography, and, of course, the particular inclinations of the family you're dealing with. These days, for instance, more and more brides are getting up to say a few words. So feel free to drop mention of this part of your practice to anyone involved in planning a wedding. You never know who's up for help when it comes to writing.

What Do I Charge?

Charge according to length—say an hour of your time for every double-spaced page.

Using the Ol' Cranium

Tiffany Owens, freelancer, Lincolnville, Maine

I've always been a pop culture princess, with a head filled with trivia, especially about music, movies, and entertainment. I received one of my favorite and most unusual assignments—writing trivia cards for the Cranium Turbo Edition game—after a former colleague of mine from MSN.com went to work for Cranium and suggested me for the job. That gig led me to write trivia cards for kids for another of Cranium's games, Cadoo. The questions were later included in Burger King's kids' meals. The best part came later, when my five-year-old niece got a Burger King kids' meal and my sister told her, "Oh, your auntie made those cards." The quizzical look on my niece's face was priceless.

LOVE POEMS

When I was eighteen, I went on one of those whirlwind Contiki trips with my best friend—you know, the kind where you're in a different European country every few days and you rarely know which country it is, but you soak up the experience just the same, and afterwards, when you're back home and you hear people say things like, "Vienna is beautiful in July," you respond by saying, "Oh, I loved Vienna when I was there one summer," even though you realize you might be picturing Barcelona.

There were something like fifty people in our tour group, so it stands to reason that over the course of six weeks a few of them might become, um, romantically inclined. This occurred in spades with Linda, a fellow Torontonian, and an Australian chap named ... let's call him Conrad, since that was his name. Linda fell hard for Conrad's puppy-dog eyes and nearly unintelligible accent, and she wanted to let him know. A few weeks into the trip, she asked if I could help write a romantic poem to Conrad on her behalf. Lesson number one: When someone asks if you can *help* them write something, you are going to end up writing the entire thing start to finish, as much because you don't want her help as because she doesn't want to give it. This works better for everyone.

After spending some time with Linda asking her what it was about Conrad that charmed her most and what she felt when she was with him, I composed a few stanzas for her to write in her own hand. This felt funny, since the only poetry I'd ever written before was my own. What made me comfortable was that Linda freely admitted to Conrad that she'd enlisted my help. She'd just wanted to capture her feelings as well as they could be captured, she told him, and he, after downing a few beers, got pretty choked up about it.

Again, I encourage you to treat such cases as professional jobs, with corresponding fees. The reason you'll receive such requests is that people recognize how valuable your talent is. Make sure you realize it, too.

86 LOVE POEMS	The more people discover you're a writer, the more you'll find them coming to you to help them express their feelings.

Get This Gig: Love Poems

Where Do I Start?

Make this particular offering a specific part of your marketing letter or brochure, or maybe create a separate tab for it on your Web site. If you think there's no appetite out there for this service, think again. Remember: Nonwriters don't like writing, nor are they good at it. Writers tend to forget that because they adore writing and it comes naturally to them.

Who Do I Contact?

Send occasional e-mail blasts to your friends, associates, clients, and prospects announcing exciting news, business promotions you're offering, and so on. Send one of these a few weeks prior to Valentine's Day and make its focus your one-time offer to ghostwrite a romantic poem for, say, a flat fee of $25. Or something to that effect. The goal here is to let people know, in a subtle way, that this is one of the things you do.

What Do I Charge?

People recruiting you to help write poetry for them are doing so because they've tried it and discovered how hard it is to do—or do well, at least. Charge what you think is fair. Most people will be glad to shell out for a poem that will melt their sweetheart.

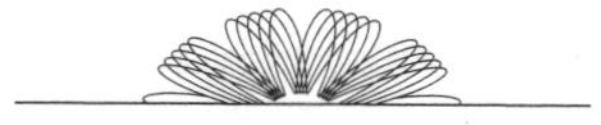

Setting Expectations

There's nothing wrong with doing work pro bono for your family members or close friends. But be careful not to set the expectation that you'll do endless work for free. You'll find that lots of people start to ask you to just glance at a letter to make sure it's okay, read their resume to see if it's up to snuff, or provide general input on their book idea to see if it's publishable. The problem is you're a writer, so you aren't going to be able to just look at a resume and tell someone it's good enough if it isn't—you're going to want to make it good enough, because you hate to see any piece of writing done poorly.

It will no doubt feel awkward and hateful at first to charge people you know, but the earlier you start to separate your business life from your personal life, the better, both for your practice and your relationships.

There are three reasons it's important to set expectations for your practice early:

1. **Almost everyone underestimates how long good writing takes.** I have an ex-colleague for whom I've written dozens of little things over the years. Early on, he'd typically send me some raw thoughts and ask me to turn them into whatever it was he needed at the time. Usually the request would be accompanied by his saying, "I figure it will take you two or three hours." I would almost always have to reply that it would in fact take me 20 percent longer than that, then I'd ask him if he still wanted me to proceed, which he always did. In underestimating my time, he wasn't deliberately trying to belittle my work; he just constantly forgot about the time it would take up front to think about and arrive at a proper structure and storyline to frame the actual writing part—the only part he was thinking about when he suggested the "two or three hours." Eventually he asked me simply to run a tab and report to him each month how much he owed. He no longer mentions how long he thinks it will take. He just asks me to make it is as good as it can be, and he trusts that I'll charge him fairly. "Easy reading is

damned hard writing," wrote Nathaniel Hawthorne, and he was damned right.

2. **It looks professional.** If you do something for free for one person and charge someone else for the same type of work, as word spreads of your practice no one will know what to expect, the unintentional consequence of which is that everyone will hope for the freebie. Naturally I'm not talking about your family or closest friends, but requests for your time from anyone else should be addressed with absolute consistency.

3. **It usually just takes once.** Anyone skeptical about the monetary value of good writing is usually converted after witnessing just one before-and-after example. So, while you may hear lots of "It really takes *that* long?" comments at first, the longer you write, the more people you write for, and the more word of mouth you generate, the less frequent such comments will become. Eventually, they'll disappear for good.

If you don't believe your time is valuable, others won't, either. So it behooves you to get into the habit of telling people, the moment they ask you to just "have a look" at their résumé, that you estimate it would take you *X* hours to improve it. That lets them know that those hours are going to entail a fee. Eventually you'll get used to this, and your practice will function a lot more successfully because you've established early on that you're a professional whose time is, like everyone else's, money.

APPLICATION ESSAYS

Both the standards and the competition surrounding academic programs seem to increase every year. Those applying for a spot must present information in two forms. One of these forms—grades—is objective.

The other form—essays—are anything-goes efforts in which people must explain, within a specific word count, why they are a better fit for the program, or more passionate about it, or more destined to be part of it, than the other seventeen zillion people applying. The essays count for a lot; ask anyone on an application committee. And because people realize how important they are, it usually scares the bejeezus out of them when they read over their own drafts, sending them straight to the door of someone who knows what they're doing. Someone like you.

Let me acknowledge the possibility that you may have an ethical issue doing work of this type. I don't. I consider it a professional service, and that's that. But if you do, I respect your choice.

87 APPLICATION ESSAYS	Application essays tend to be much more of a struggle than people assume they'll be—which is why they often see writers as precious resources.

Get This Gig: Application Essays

Where Do I Start?

If you know of a friend or acquaintance applying to a program, offer to have a look at his application package pro bono. Then, once you've impressed the pants off him, tell him you wouldn't mind it a bit if he wanted to tell others about your potential to help.

Who Do I Contact?

Let people know about this part of your practice individually. It will be by nature a private activity.

What Do I Charge?

Use good judgment when determining which end of your pay scale to use for these assignments. On one hand, the use of your skills can prove pivotal. On the other, people applying to academic programs aren't usually rolling in money. Be fair but conservative.

ACADEMIC PAPERS

There's the issue of getting into the program, and then there's the issue of doing well once you're in. A nonwriter's troubles hardly end once application essays are in the rearview mirror. In fact, they've only just begun, because looming now are multiple deadlines for, depending on the program, various types of writing assignments, from business cases to reports to essays. Want to see the picture of despair? Watch someone who doesn't enjoy writing working on an academic dissertation. In such cases, you're pretty close to a superhero—Writerman, perhaps—swooping in to help save the day. Again, you may or may not feel comfortable pursuing work of this sort.

88 ACADEMIC PAPERS	Academic writing requires discipline, the ability to make cogent arguments, and adherence to structure. Such things are probably second nature to you—not so to others.

Get This Gig: Academic Papers

Where Do I Start?

If you've written academic papers before, you've already got your start. This isn't a service you want to broadcast explicitly, nor will the people who enlist you to write them want to make it public knowledge that they're getting your help. But feel free to mention it in conversation.

Who Do I Contact?

No one actively. They'll come to you.

What Do I Charge?

Not unduly little—good academic writing takes time. Two hours per page is a fair base rate.

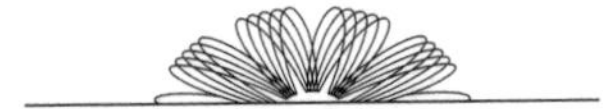

Casket Copy

Paula Hubbs Cohen, freelancer, Phoenix, Arizona

Today I'm a full-time freelancer specializing in writing marketing copy and feature articles about luxury homes and properties. But as with most writers, when I was more of a neophyte I was scrambling for any assignment in any industry. One day, and I honestly don't recall the full cycle of events, I stumbled across an assignment that I eventually won: writing about various aspects of the funeral industry. For example, I had to research laws regarding the interstate sale of caskets, including information from the Federal Trade Commission and the National Funeral Directors Association. I also learned about funeral home software, Casket Price Lists (referred to in the industry as CPL)—and about the fact that you can order a casket online, including from Costco. I'm serious! Just go to the Costco Web site and click on "Funeral." You can even get expedited shipping. To this day, when the subject of funerals comes up, most people don't believe me when I tell them you can order a casket from Costco and have it shipped overnight.

LINER NOTES

For a long time I would read the liner notes contained in the music CDs I bought and wonder who'd written them. Some of them were quite good; some left me thinking I could do better. Then I happened to connect with an ex-classmate who had become the marketing manager at a music production company. Today, one of my most enjoyable ongoing challenges is writing liner notes for the CDs they produce, a diverse array of albums ranging from classic artist compilations to hits from specific eras to interpretive nature compositions. Their creative director usually provides pretty detailed creative briefs, so I know in general what I need to deliver, but they also give me a lot of latitude, making both the research and the brainstorming thoroughly pleasurable. The notes are usually 250 words or less, so they need to capture a certain mood while being entertaining, informative, and accessible to a broad audience. Plus I get to listen to music as part of my work.

Once, they asked me to write notes for a country album. I wasn't sure I could deliver an authentic note, because I assumed I didn't like country music. I put the CD on, closed my eyes, and waited to see if I'd have a reaction. You know what? After a few bars of "Coal Miner's Daughter," I was hooked. So I'm thankful to this client for expanding my personal horizons, too. They still haven't sold me on hip-hop, but you never know.

Music and writing—can you think of a better combination not involving chocolate?

Get This Gig: Liner Notes

Where Do I Start?

Take out all your music CDs, open the jewel cases, and read the liner notes for those that have them. Make a note of the companies that produce those CDs. Then prepare a version of your introductory letter that includes mention of liner notes.

Who Do I Contact?

Call the company's office, identify yourself quickly as a professional writer, and ask the receptionist if you could please speak to someone about the possibility of writing liner notes. Acceptable responses are someone's name, voice mail, or e-mail address. Keep at it until you get one of those, then get in touch.

What Do I Charge?

Bill an hourly rate combining the writing itself and any research that may be required. For the 250-word notes I write, I charge three hours for the writing plus any research time.

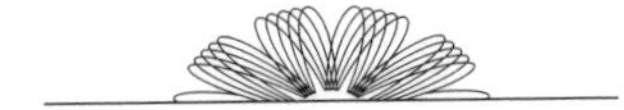

Now That's What You Call DEVOTED WRITING

Brandy Brow, freelancer, southern Vermont

While searching LinkedIn for members near my town, I found a person who had graduated from my high school who also happened to be in the arts/music/writing field and, like me, a Christian. I introduced myself as a fellow alumnus and invited him to read my profile. In a few messages I learned that he happened to be a key person from one of my early childhood memories: the teenage boy I saw one time standing with his bicycle outside my grandfather's art shop in the foyer of a large building when I was about five. We both found it interesting, and apparently he also found my profile interesting. He requested devotional writing samples, and I landed a job you don't find on the market—writing thirty meditations for songs by popular Christian artists, now appearing in the CD and devotional book set *Songs of Hope for the Hurting Heart*.

GREETING CARDS

Companies like Hallmark and American Greetings are constantly on the lookout for freelance writers who can come up with clever new angles for all of the different occasions their cards address—Valentine's Day, Mother's Day, the holidays, births, graduations, weddings, anniversaries, and on and on. I wouldn't be surprised if you've spent some time browsing greeting card racks, decidedly underwhelmed by the number of mediocre cards you come across. Nor would I be surprised if you could do better.

90 GREETING CARDS	Greeting cards can be a surprisingly competitive area, but it's worth the effort of gaining entry, because they're virtually recession-proof.

Get This Gig: Greeting Cards

Where Do I Start?

Browse the racks of greetings cards at your local bookstore or gift store. Look at the ones you feel most closely match your tone and style. Turn the cards over, find out who produces them, and contact the companies directly to find out how you can submit some ideas. Also, look in your copy of *Writer's Market* under the section called Greeting Cards, which lists over twenty markets.

Who Do I Contact?

Go to the Web sites of the companies whose cards you selected and those listed in *Writer's Market*. Some of them will list writer's guidelines. For those that don't, call their offices and ask.

What Do I Charge?

Most companies pay from $25 to $150 for each idea they buy. Some pay as much as $500 for a single idea or verse.

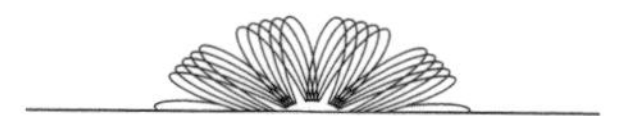

Taking the Grant **BY THE HORNS**

Sue Chehrenegar, freelancer, Culver City, California

While attending weekly City Council meetings as a reporter for the local paper, I learned about a request for proposals. I had recently taken a grant writing course, and I felt certain that a local restaurant owner would be interested in going after the available grant. I spoke with him about the possibility of my writing a proposal on his behalf. He agreed. After two meetings, I showed him the final proposal. He had me deliver it for him, and I made $200.

P2P CORRESPONDENCE

There's this ex-colleague of mine. He's one of the busiest people I know and also one of the most tactical. He holds firm to the belief that he should deal with the things he does well and recruit help for everything else. To that end, he's had me write dozens of things for him. Often he'll ask for my help composing e-mails to colleagues, friends, or others—what I call his P2P, or Personal to Personal, correspondence, because he doesn't necessarily trust himself to get the tone and feel just right. In soliciting my help, he isn't trying to sound falsely writerly; he just wants to ensure his personal communications achieve what they're supposed to. I admire this attitude, I enjoy helping him, and he never for a moment balks at paying me for every minute of my time he uses.

Recently, he realized that he and his wife were having to write a lot of cards—thank-you cards from their own wedding, congratulatory cards for births or other people's weddings or anniversaries, condolence cards—and he didn't feel their true feelings were being done justice because they were such average writers. So he asked if I could prepare for him a series of templates they could use for different occasions that would help them deliver stronger, more heartfelt sentiments. I created three frameworks each for four different types of event: births, anniversaries, weddings, and deaths. The three frameworks corresponded to different relationship levels—the first for loose or peripheral acquaintances, the second for steadier relationships, the third for intimate family or friends.

When approached with an assignment like this, remind yourself not to treat it lightly. I worked extremely hard developing the templates for my ex-colleague and his wife because I knew how important it was to him, and I also knew that he viewed me as his go-to guy for any of his writing or compositional needs. If I want to maintain this status, I'd better not take it for granted. That means treating every request he brings me no differently than if it were accompanied by a purchase order, a confidentiality agreement, and a contract signed in septuplicate.

91 P2P CORRESPONDENCE	Because personal requests naturally feel more casual, they can also seem less important. But they can engender the kind of loyalty that ends up just as lasting, and wide-ranging, as the most secure contract.

Get This Gig: P2P Correspondence

Where Do I Start?

There are two ways to approach P2P writing. The first is secondary promotion: Once you've done more typical writing work for someone, send a follow-up communication listing all the other types of services you offer, including P2P. The second is primary promotion: Actively publicize it in your standard marketing letter or kit.

Who Do I Contact?

Everyone has personal writing needs, and sometimes the only reason they haven't paid a writer to help is because they haven't realized there's one available. Using the primary or secondary approach, announce your services through every channel possible to everyone who will listen.

What Do I Charge?

P2P work should be billed at the low end of your hourly rate.

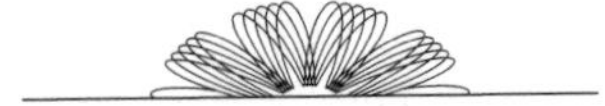

There's Research, and THEN THERE'S RESEARCH

Casey A. Johnson, freelancer, Dundas, Canada

> The first year I was in business, I was approached by a woman looking for a skilled writer. After some initial discussion and a review of my portfolio, she said she wanted to hire me because of my journalism training and writing skills. The next thing I knew I was working as a part-time licensed private investigator taking statements from witnesses on high-profile cases. After several months, I was happy to give it up, as some of the statements I took included testimony against some rather unsavory characters, and I didn't fancy being part of the witness relocation program under the heading of "Ticked off too many bad guys"—but it was certainly an interesting experience.

WORDS

Literally, individual words. If your mom calls you because she can't think of a particular word, sending her a bill might be inappropriate. But consider that for every fifteen minutes of work many lawyers do, they bill an hour. No, I'm not aiming to match people's perceptions of writers to that of lawyers. But small requests tend to have a way of growing into larger ones, so I want you to manage people's expectations in a strategic fashion.

What I mean is this. Someone calls you because they can't come up with a word. "It's like that thing where you feel two different ways about something, or you're like on the fence about it but not really, you know?" As a writer, you know full well that one can't just pluck a word out of the air without knowing what kind of sentence it's being inserted into or what kind of piece of writing that sentence is a part of. So you ask the person to read you the whole sentence for context. "Let me just e-mail you the whole thing," he says. "You don't have to read it all, but it'll be easier this way. I'll highlight the part where I need the word. If you want, you can tell me if you think it's any good or if I should change any parts." Two minutes later you've received in your e-mail inbox a five-paragraph letter the person has drafted to send to his local congressman regarding a proposal to place speed bumps along the length of his street.

The one elusive word aside, the letter is filled with room for improvement. Your instinct is, of course, to work on the whole thing. Don't. That creates the expectation that you'll do it again next time, and the time after that. Without making any changes, suggest a word in the highlighted spot, and, if you feel comfortable doing so, include a note in your return e-mail that says something like, "For future reference, I can always put in an hour or two on documents like this to get them just right if you'd like. My normal rate is $80 per hour, but for you it's $60." And then don't be surprised if you get asked to put in that hour or two right then and there. This might seem distasteful to you at first, but in the long run you'll be glad you've established suitable expectations, even for "small" requests.

92 WORDS	Establish suitable expectations even for "small" requests—it will serve you well in the long run.

Get This Gig: Words

Where Do I Start?

Most critical is that you firmly establish the parameters of your business. It's important to send the implicit message that *all* of your work is billable. This way, people will never assume you're going to do something free for them, and when you do, they'll be doubly happy about it.

Who Do I Contact?

The sky's the limit. Let everyone know you're here to help with words, whether one word or a thousand.

What Do I Charge?

In the case of someone truly asking for a single word and no more, don't charge—at least not the first time. If it happens multiple times, gently explain that you're going to have to charge. In the more common case where that word needs to be considered in the context of an entire piece, and that piece needs to be looked at, too, charge an hourly rate. Just be clear what you're charging for.

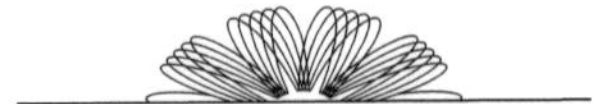

And From the "YOU REALLY NEVER KNOW WHERE WORK IS GOING TO COME FROM" FILE ...

Annika S. Hipple, freelancer, Seattle, Washington

I recently got an out-of-the-blue request from an English-language newspaper in the United Arab Emirates to write an article for their House & Home section. They wanted to profile a home interiors store in Seattle for their weekly "Cult Shop" feature. I suspect they had run a search for Seattle freelance writers and found me through my profile on Biznik, a social networking site that does a lot better in Google than my own site (the profile then has a link to my Web site). It was fun to get an unexpected assignment from halfway around the world!

P2B CORRESPONDENCE

A letter to a congressman is an example of what I call P2B, or Personal to Business, correspondence—letters people write or e-mails they send to companies, ministries, government, institutions, chambers of commerce, or any other professional organization or person affiliated with one. People write such things all the time, and they're constantly frustrated by their inability to say something as forcefully as they wish they could.

P2B correspondence ranges widely. An associate of yours might be writing a strongly worded letter to the Ministry of Transportation to challenge its wanting to suspend his license due to a rash of unpaid parking tickets. Perhaps a soon-to-be-graduating schoolmate has asked some of her professors for reference letters, and each one of them has told her to write whatever she wants and then bring it to them for signing, but she has no idea what to write or how to make it sound convincing while not over the top. Or maybe one of your friends is just dying to compose the perfect letter to Oprah about why she'd be an ideal guest on the show.

93 P2B CORRESPONDENCE	People are constantly frustrated by their inability to say things to businesses as persuasively as they'd like. Enter you.

Get This Gig: P2B Correspondence

Where Do I Start?

Make people aware of your services by sending out professional, properly thought-out letters, brochures, or marketing kits that allude to all the things you want people to realize they might need help with.

Who Do I Contact?

Anyone and everyone.

What Do I Charge?

For this type of work, charge an hourly rate that's lower than your corporate rate but not so low that it isn't worth your while.

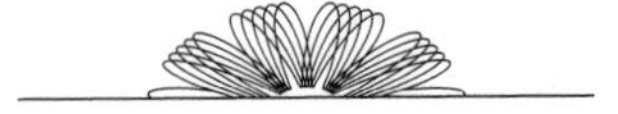

Starbucks Serendipity

Avil Beckford, freelancer, Toronto, Canada

A couple of years ago I met with the president of an association that I am a member of. I usually meet her for coffee a couple times a year to update her on what I'm doing and to find out what's new in the association. During that particular meeting, at a Starbucks in downtown Toronto, I told her that I was writing my first book, *Tales of People Who Get It*, and explained to her that I'd used interviews to gather my information. She became quite excited and said, "I have a project for you, let's go to the office." It turns out that the next year the association was celebrating its fifteenth anniversary and wanted to profile fifteen of its members in an anniversary booklet. My associate was also a subscriber to my newsletter, in which I present one interview of a highly accomplished individual each month. So my newsletter, coupled with the book, demonstrated that I was qualified for the project. The anniversary booklet turned out great, everyone was happy, and the association continues to use it when seeking funding for its programs because they feel the profiles are compelling. Talk about finding a project in an unexpected place!

RADIO SCRIPTS

Television depends on pictures, and radio depends on words. Call-in shows, news programs, the "spontaneous" banter between deejays, the simple life truths shared by your favorite easy-listening host—all of it gets written somewhere, by someone.

94

RADIO SCRIPTS

Radio depends on words. Some of those words are spontaneous, but the rest need to be written.

Get This Gig: Radio Scripts

Where Do I Start?

Spend time listening to a few of your local stations and key in on the nonspontaneous stuff you hear—the stuff that sounds like it's been scripted. Then check out books like *Writing for Radio* by Rosemary Horstmann to get smart about the process. Radio producers and directors are fast-paced people accustomed to having quick conversations and making fast decisions, so a letter isn't an effective way to approach them. Prepare a verbal pitch of thirty seconds to one minute that outlines your interest in writing for radio and the qualifications and/or special skills you bring to the table.

Who Do I Contact?

Get in touch with the stations you've been listening to, ask to speak to a producer, and make some general inquiries: You're a local professional writer, you love the radio business and are looking for writing opportunities within it, do they have any writing/scripting needs, and so on.

What Do I Charge?

Rates for radio writing vary widely depending on your credentials, what you're writing, and who you're writing it for.

Exercising YOUR OPTIONS

Jan Yager, freelancer, Stamford, Connecticut

I was working full-time as an editorial assistant at Macmillan publishing in its school division, but I wanted to be a writer of my own work. During lunch hours, I took an exercise class at the Y near the company's office in midtown Manhattan. While we were doing our jumping jacks, another class member and I started talking. She shared that she'd just become editor of a new magazine on Long Island and was looking for freelance writers, and I shared that I was looking for writing assignments. She asked me to send her a query. I queried and got an assignment, "Who's Who on East Hampton," which led to a second. One of the assignments was to interview famous artists who lived in East Hampton; the other was to interview famous actors and actresses. The magazine, called *Paumanok*, no longer exists, but because of it I went on to sell articles to *Parade*, *Opera News*, the op-ed page of *The New York Times*, *Newsday*, and, ultimately, twenty-six books translated into twenty-two languages, and counting.

TV SCRIPTS

You know that sitcom you watch every week? If you take all the lines of dialogue and add them together, they amount to somewhere in the neighborhood of just a couple thousand words.

Of course, the words are incredibly precise, and they've probably been worked over a dozen times or more before actually getting to the tube. The important thing to remember is that they, and the rest of the script (like scene details), came originally from some writer's head and were typed and submitted by that writer, and she is now enjoying residuals every time the episode is aired.

TV writing has always carried a special allure. Though it's hard work, it's also undeniably fun, and there is a certain prestige that goes with having TV credits as a notch in your writing belt.

95 TV SCRIPTS	To get into TV writing, you need to write spec scripts, and then you need to get those scripts into someone's hands.

Get This Gig: TV Scripts

Where Do I Start?

At one time, TV shows were written almost exclusively by freelancers; today they're written mostly by in-house staff, but most of those people only became staff in the first place because they were freelancers who wrote so well that the shows hired them full-time.

To write for television you need to generate a few sample scripts. These are referred to in the business as "spec" scripts (as in "written on speculation"—as opposed to commissioned), and their sole purpose is to demonstrate your ability as a potential TV writer. They aren't scripts you hope or expect will actually get produced; they're your calling card, created to show your writing chops. A spec script can be for an existing show or for a show from your own imagination. For a half-hour sitcom, spec scripts are around twenty-two to twenty-seven pages. Script format is specific, so if you aren't familiar with it, Google some sample TV scripts, buy a book on scriptwriting, or invest in script writing software so the template is laid out and all you have to do is fill in the words.

In general, producers want to see a few different samples so they can be convinced of your versatility. Submitting two spec scripts together is an acceptable industry norm, but it's a good idea to have others in your back pocket, too, in case the request for more should come. There's no magic formula or secret shortcut for writing the right TV script. Most insiders still say what they always have: To write a great spec script, at least for an existing show, get to know the show inside-out, develop as deep a feel for it as you can, read produced scripts of the series (available via a simple Web search these days), and then set to the task of writing your own, aiming to make it at least as good as the ones you watch week in and week out, if not, in your opinion, better.

Who Do I Contact?

Getting your spec scripts into people's hands can be a tricky little song and dance, but script submitting is, in the end, no different from, say, short story submitting. Producers, like editors, are always hoping to stumble on writers of serious talent, and good scripts will eventually land in front of a pair of eyes attached to a person who matters. If you don't have a contact of your own—someone who knows someone who knows someone else who can forward the script to someone in the industry with the power to hire writers—send a letter to the Writers Guild of America (WGA) asking for a complete list of current contacts at existing series and use it as your basis for submitting. You might also consider registering your material with the WGA, or at least mailing it to yourself and keeping it sealed so you have proof of its being written by you on a certain date.

Should someone see your spec submissions and like them, several things might happen. First, she might ask for other samples. As I said, be ready to send those. Second, she might invite you in for a pitch session, a meeting in which you'll be expected to present more ideas for episodes or storylines. Third, she might offer to buy (or "option") one of the spec scripts. This is the long shot—but it's happened to others, so there's no reason to believe it can't happen to you, too.

What Do I Charge?

For TV writing, you don't set the rates; they do.

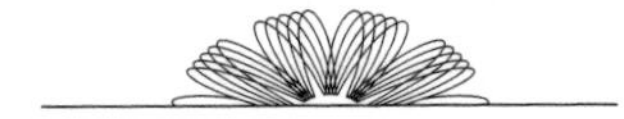

Answering the Question

Friends familiar with your long-time desire to write may good-naturedly tease you about the risk of giving up your thankless but stable nine-to-five grind to tackle something so daunting. Former colleagues may wonder aloud about your decision. Busybody aunts will gossip about how no one makes money writing and what a nice doctor or lawyer you would have made (nor will they stop no matter how successful you become).

Change their perception by embracing and celebrating your decision rather than timidly defending it. When people ask, "So what are you doing now?," answer with pride and conviction. Don't say, "I thought I'd give freelancing a go and see how it works out" or "I'm going to try being a freelance writer, though I'm not sure what that means." Have your elevator speech—a business term for the thirty-second spiel that describes what you do—always at the ready. When people ask me what I do, I respond, "I'm a freelance writer and communications consultant." If they want to know more, I tell them my practice is divided evenly between journalism, like newspaper features, and corporate writing, which entails everything from marketing brochures to ghostwriting business books. Suddenly they're intrigued. They see writing as a real, viable, honest-to-goodness business—not because I've given them my income statement but because I've spoken about it in a clear, confident manner.

Let's stop apologizing for being writers. I love being one, and I bet you do, too. Tell anyone who asks.

SONG LYRICS

In the music industry, singer-songwriters are the exception, not the norm. Sheryl Crow, a popular female performer, got her start when a catchy little pop tune, "All I Wanna Do," exploded during the mid-1990s, launching an award-winning career that, as I write this, is ten albums strong and counting. Did you know that the lyrics for "All I Wanna Do" were based on a poem? One day, Crow's producer Bill Bottrell was browsing Cliff's Books, a used bookstore in Pasadena, when he came upon a poetry collection called *The Country of Here Below* by Wyn Cooper. Bottrell sent the volume to Crow, who adapted one of the poems, "Fun," into the song she happened to be working on at the time. The song took off, and Cooper, whose book had an initial press run of five hundred copies, saw it go into multiple reprints instead—not to mention the considerable royalties.

Elton John, it is well known, owes his legendary career in large part to a modest lad from Lincolnshire, England, who had a flair for writing lyrics. When Bernie Taupin was seventeen, he answered an ad for talent placed in the *New Musical Express* by Liberty Records and submitted some of the lines he'd written. These were passed along to Reginald Kenneth Dwight, a new singer Liberty had on its roster, and the rest, as they say, is history. As you smile each time the familiar refrains of "Rocket Man," "Tiny Dancer," or "Your Song" come on the radio, remember that the singer wrote the music, but someone else wrote the words.

Music companies are always alert not just for those with special voices but also those who can compose a tune or write a lyric. If you think writing lyrics is up your alley, go ahead and call some music companies and ask whether they consider submissions. Because in this business, you never know unless you ask.

96 SONG LYRICS	For every musician who writes his own material, there are dozens of recording artists whose songs consist of melodies—and lyrics—written by others.

Get This Gig: Song Lyrics

Where Do I Start?

Almost any kind of writing can work as lyrics—rhyming poetry, nonrhyming poetry, straight prose, experimental prose (Leonard Cohen, anyone?), letters, missives, scat phrases ... even single lines can carry virtually an entire song (see George Harrison's "I Got My Mind Set On You"). Of course, there's no law against sitting down to consciously write song lyrics.

Who Do I Contact?

One option is to submit lyrics to the music companies themselves. Call and ask who entertains such submissions. You can also send your stuff directly to musical artists—usually through their managers or agents, whose contact information you should be able to find on the Web without too much trouble. Finally, you can actively publicize your lyric-writing services. Those adept at writing music but poor with words might just be happy to find you.

What Do I Charge?

If a music production company or established artist wants to use your lyrics, they'll likely make an offer based on their own set of rates. Don't be afraid to negotiate. Once you've sold those rights, they're sold for good, and, as in the case of Sheryl Crow above, you never know which song is going to blast off.

For your own lyric-writing services, charge a flat rate. A few hundred dollars per song is about right, depending on the length of the song and the complexity of the tune.

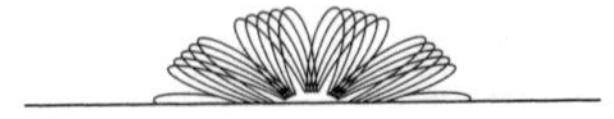

Culinary Characters

Serenity J. Knutson, freelancer, Brookings, South Dakota

While I make my living as a full-time writer/editor, I also moonlight, on occasion, as a server for some friends in the restaurant business. I quickly grew accustomed to the requests to proofread the new menu designs, but then one recent day I was asked to write a full-length feature article on the history of the restaurant for its fiftieth anniversary.

KID STUFF

Happily included in my usual stack of bills and junk mail today was the new issue of *Chirp*, a terrifically fun magazine written for three-to-six-year-olds. My four-year-old son Oliver adores it. In each issue there are a few stories, a couple of poems, some activities, animal facts, jokes, puzzles, and contests. A lot of content gets packed into a relatively small magazine, and I've noticed two important things: Bylines are never repeated within the same issue, and you don't usually see the same ones appear from issue to issue, either. That means different freelancers are contributing content all the time.

The same can be said for other kids' media. The four episodes of the *Franklin the Turtle* DVD Oliver just received from his grandparents were each written by a different person. These episodes aren't short—fifteen minutes per, in fact. Someone got paid a nice buck to make sure Franklin and Bear patched things up after having that disagreement about the paper sailboat.

Even though the kid-related slice of the writing pie is a significant one—there's a reason *Children's Writer's & Illustrator's Market* contains over four hundred pages—it tends not to register on most writers' radar screens until they have children themselves, because (a) that's when they become immersed in all things kid-related, including literature, and (b) that's when they become most strongly inclined to write stuff for children, since they're around the little scamps all the time and therefore percolating with ideas to keep them entertained.

Kid-focused writing may seem easy at first blush because it appears basic in structure, light in theme, and straightforward in language. But most writers, upon tackling it for the first time, find it harder than they assumed. Go easy on yourself, then, if you find your early attempts at writing for children lacking. Those little tykes are a demanding audience, but an appreciative one, too, so it's worth the effort to get it right.

97

KID STUFF

Think editors of adult publications are happy when they find a writer they can depend on? Editors of kids' publications are over the moon.

Get This Gig: Kid Stuff

Where Do I Start?

Head to your nearest bookstore and spend some time in the children's section. If you've never entered before, you might be stunned to find how plentiful it is with books, magazines, toys, videos, and lots of other neat-o stuff. Which of them spark you? Which ones do you connect with?

Do some thinking, over the course of several days, about the kinds of stories you think would be fun to write. You probably need look no further than your own life. A great proportion of popular children's stories come from the authors' experiences with their own little ones. Maybe that time your daughter ate the crayon would make a good story about parental tolerance. Your son's mix of anger and frustration over never having scored a goal in soccer could be fodder for a tale about how every kid has different talents. And so on.

Who Do I Contact?

If you want to write for kids' magazines, contact the editors. If you want to write kids' books, contact the publishers. If you're looking to hook up with a toy company or kids' retailer, get contact information either from their products or their Web site, and then ask what opportunities are available. If you want to write scripts for kids, contact TV, movie, or video production companies.

What Do I Charge?

For existing kids' channels and outlets, rates will already be set. But there's nothing stopping you from creating your own kids' materials—

parents are *always* on the lookout for stuff to help occupy their little ones—and attaching a cost.

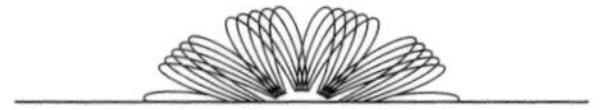

Assume You Can Do It, THEN FIGURE OUT HOW

When new or unusual work suddenly comes your way, it can be intimidating. There's a certain comfort we all derive from writing the same type of article many times over or editing a report for a company with whose practices we're intimately familiar.

But try not to say no too quickly in these situations—not until you've given the opportunity due consideration, at least. You can tackle it if anyone can. Plus, the project might just end up taking you out on an exciting new branch that becomes a permanent part of your writing tree.

In the same vein, don't ever dismiss a project as something you would never, ever take on or a certain genre or form as something you would never, ever pursue. Throughout your writing journey, new ideas and assignments will present themselves to you from out of nowhere, and the fact that they scare you a little should be all the reason you need to embrace them for all they're worth. Dip your toe in and see what it feels like. Then wade in a little further. And a little further ...

EROTICA

The purpose of this book is to let you know about *all* the opportunities available for writers, so let's talk not just about children's fare but also the stuff that would fall at the other end of the spectrum—sexy writing. Don't scoff until you've actually taken a shot at erotic writing. It's easy to write poorly, not so easy to write well. If you can cage it effectively, however, there are numerous points of entry you might take advantage of. From online zines to soft-core pornography scripts (or full-bore hard-core, if that's your thing—Lord knows they could use competent writers), erotica as much as any other genre highlights the enormous discrepancy between good writing and bad. Because of this discrepancy, well-written erotica tends to stand out from the pack.

98 EROTICA	As erotica in all its forms becomes increasingly mainstream, the need for those who can write decent erotica increases.

Get This Gig: Erotica

Where Do I Start?

Erotica can be found in more places than ever before, including television, books, magazines, and online (in case you didn't know). The advantages are that (a) it's a lot easier to find than it used to be, and (b) it's no longer underground. Check out the index in your copy of *Writer's Market* to find places where erotica finds print these days, and do some online surfing, too. Obviously when you search "erotica" online you're going to come across, um, lots of different varieties to consider, but it's also going to show you the extent to which erotica has entered the mainstream and the many ways in which it's currently packaged. Like I said, there are lots of badly written erotica out there, so if you can do a good job of it, there are lots of opportunities available. If you don't believe me, just tune in to some late-night Cinemax. I'm serious.

Who Do I Contact?

Depending on what kind of erotica you want to write, target your search to magazine editors, book editors, online editors, TV producers, or, if you're inclined to go that route, production companies like Vivid that specialize in erotica.

What Do I Charge?

Rates for erotic writing will be mostly established, but, based on your credentials, feel free to haggle as much as you feel is appropriate.

Eight Ball, CORNER POCKET

Meryl K. Evans, freelancer, Plano, Texas

A number of unexpected writing assignments have come my way. Becoming a columnist for *PC Today* magazine was one. A guy I hadn't talked to in ages (we worked together on a Web site) referred them to me, and I wrote for them until they stopped freelancing. Another was doing an annual column for *Billiards Digest*, which was particularly amusing since I don't play pool at all. The editor found me online and I've worked with them for three years. But the most unusual is probably writing the copy for a board game called Fib-or-Not? I don't remember how the owner found me, but get this: His daughter and my sons go to the same elementary school. We live within a mile of each other.

ONLINE CONTENT

So what's your default home page? MSN? CNN? ESPN? National Geographic Online? Google Earth? Whatever it is, I bet you check it every time you log on and spend a few minutes (or more—shhh) clicking through a link or three before settling down into your real work. You're not alone. This collective tendency is powerful and on the ascent. People are on their computers around the clock, and the degree to which they get their information and entertainment online is growing by leaps and bounds on a virtually daily basis.

The related outcome to all this compulsive surfing follows the standard supply-and-demand equation. The more people look to the Web, and the more variety they demand of their online substance, the more of it needs to get produced. And the more of it gets produced, the more words need to be written. Who writes words? Writers do. I know over a dozen former print magazine editors who now specialize in online writing or editing. When they find someone who can write for an online audience, they stick with that writer. Given the lightning growth rate of the industry, no editor wants to work with any kind of writer except the kind who is as reliable and adaptable as she is innately talented.

99
ONLINE CONTENT

Online editors everywhere are talking about how desperate the need is for good writers who also understand the particular nuances of writing for the Web: straightforward style, extra concision, accessible voice, an ability to embed natural breaks, and so on.

Get This Gig: Online Content

Where Do I Start?

Online freelance opportunities are almost endless, and are also, at least at the moment, part of a continuously and rapidly expanding universe. To pursue these opportunities, search Web sites for contact information and then proceed as you would with any query, sending information about yourself along with a few writing samples and a few sentences about your interest in the particular site you'd like to write for. Online editors are no less busy than print editors these days—one might argue they're even busier—so getting responses from them can sometimes be just as challenging, but be your normal tenacious self and, eventually, someone's going to open the door.

Who Do I Contact?

Most online sites have editors just like magazines do. The better-organized sites will have something like a masthead visible somewhere on the main page, so it shouldn't be hard to find an editor's name. His contact information won't usually be included, though, so go to the Contact Us tab, call the phone number provided, and ask for the editor's e-mail address. Just the fact that you were able to get it in the first place shows the editor that you know how to dig up information.

What Do I Charge?

Online writing rates are a source of vehement current debate. Because Web sites don't generate the same degree of advertising revenue as traditional print, freelance rates for online writing are considerably low down in the pecking order—at least for now. It isn't atypical to be offered twenty-five cents per word for online writing. Usually there's some room for negotiation, but not much.

But we've promised to think long term and big picture, right? The Web is only going to continue to grow, and people are only going to continue to rely on it more, and therefore online writers are only going to become more valued and better paid. Don't dwell on the present rates you're offered for online writing. Think instead about the value of getting in today so you have consistent online gigs tomorrow.

The Glamorous Life

Brooke Kelley, freelancer, Los Angeles, California

Amazingly, one of my first clients was *Glamour* magazine. It was really unexpected seeing as how I never wrote them a query or approached them to write anything. I knew someone who knew someone who worked with the magazine, and he put me in touch with her. She wrote to me looking for interview subjects, so I gave her a few quotes for her stories. Then one day she got swamped with work, and because of our online communication, she knew I was a freelancer. I hadn't said that I was trying to work with the magazine and wasn't staying in touch with her for that reason. I was just trying to help her with her work. Anyway, she couldn't finish a project she had started, and she got permission to pass it off to me. I did the gig, and they liked my work so much, they asked me back again, and again, and again, until I was working with them on a weekly basis for four years solid. Eventually I started guest blogging for glamour.com. You never know where it's going to come from.

LEGAL ARGUMENTS

You know how, on all those TV shows about lawyers, the opening arguments always seem so masterful, the closing statements always so brilliant? I mean, don't they? First of all, most real-life legal statements don't quite achieve that level of drama and pithiness. However, whether they do or not, often they aren't written by the lawyers themselves, but someone else. It isn't easy to take reams of facts, mix it with a bit of conjecture and assumption, and spin it all into a brief address that can sway the opinions of twelve people, or at least one judge, in one direction or the other. And for many people—most lawyers included—it isn't just not easy, it's downright excruciating. Writers, of course, welcome such a test.

100 LEGAL ARGUMENTS	Writing a good legal argument isn't so much about knowing the ins and outs of the law as it is about taking a complex story and making it seem simple.

Get This Gig: Legal Arguments

Where Do I Start?

Draft a version of your introductory letter tailored specifically to law firms. Let them know about your general services, but emphasize also the specific skill of writing legal arguments. Think about offering the

first one pro bono. Most legal firms handle a lot of volume, so one good demonstration of your talent might translate into a lot of paid work.

Who Do I Contact?

Start with legal firms in your area. Contact firms of various sizes to see which are the most responsive. If none of the Big Dogs respond but half of the Small Fish do, for example, you know where to concentrate your efforts.

What Do I Charge?

Lawyers live in the world of, um, healthy fees, so they shouldn't experience much sticker shock. Not that you should be trying to gouge them unfairly. As always, you want to try to maximize your earning power while avoiding pricing yourself out of a project. Approach it the way they themselves would: Let them know your hourly rate and charge accordingly.

MENUS

I'm serious. Think for a moment about how many restaurants there are—in your town, or the next town, or the closest metropolitan center. Now think about how persuasive good menus sound and how boring poor ones sound. Not to mention those stories that sometimes appear as part of the menu, usually involving the history of the place or the family that owns and/or started it. I can tell you most restaurateurs don't write those stories all by themselves. Menus change all the time, new restaurants open constantly, and their owners are looking for any tiny advantage that will help them avoid the usual fate of new restaurant ventures. Menus that sound great can be one of those advantages.

Restaurant owners are looking for any tiny advantage that will help them avoid the typical fate of new restaurants. Menus that sing can be one of those advantages.

Get This Gig: Menus

Where Do I Start?

Do a little reconnaissance work. Visit a bunch of restaurants and make notes about their menus, including possible suggestions you'd make for improvement.

Who Do I Contact?

Once you're done, dressed in your professional duds, personally visit each of the restaurants whose menus you feel could stand improvement, and ask to speak to the owner. In one minute or less, introduce yourself, provide your business card, and mention with a smile and a friendly tone that you happened to be dining there earlier in the week, noticed an area of two in which the menu might be worked on, and, as a professional wordsmith, would be happy to lend a hand if he'd like.

What Do I Charge?

Don't talk cost during that initial conversation. If and when you receive a phone call or e-mail, say something like, "Thanks for getting in touch, Mr. Joseph. I'd be happy to take a look at your menu. Would you like me to send you an estimate for this work?" If you get a positive response, have a look at the menu and determine a quote you think is worthwhile to you and within the appetite (so to speak) of your potential client.

GRANTS

There are always many people, groups, and companies looking for extra cash flow to help achieve their immediate and long-term goals. This extra cash can sometimes be found in the form of government grants, bursaries, subsidies, or endowments, all of which require applications that typically include lots of writing.

102
GRANTS

When trying to win a grant of, say, $10,000, most organizations will be happy to invest a few hundred dollars for the skills of a professional writer.

Get This Gig: Grants

Where Do I Start?

It will be difficult to know which companies are aware of, or applying for, which grants, so simply include "grant writing" as one of the services you name in your introductory communication. It's the kind of thing that stands out, so if a company happens to receive your letter at the same time they're applying for a grant or considering doing so, you've established a strong starting point.

Who Do I Contact?

Send your letter to both the company's human resources manager and its accounting manager or CFO.

What Do I Charge?

You may be required to do significant up-front work getting to know the company and the specific reasons it needs—and, in the sponsoring agency's eyes, deserves—the grant. In addition, some applications are quite brief and simple, and others quite long and involved. As always, ask as many questions as possible at the outset in order to fully understand expectations on both sides—then quote whatever you think is fair plus 20 percent.

INDEX